DIVIDEND

INVESTING

THE ULTIMATE BEGINNERS GUIDE TO GENERATE PASSIVE INCOME INVESTING IN THE STOCK MARKET, BONDS, OPTIONS, ETFS. FIND SAFE, CASH FLOW PRODUCING INVESTMENTS WITH HIGH RETURNS

MARK SWING

TABLE OF CONTENT

INTRODUCTION

The popularity of dividend investment is because investors prefer a stable steam of income as dividends. In addition, they reinvest these earnings to purchase more stocks. The business models of these companies are usually quite strong and their share price is likely to increase further. In addition, these well-established organizations often provide dividends on an annual basis, For example, there has been an increase in the dividends of 3M for the past 59 years, while the past five years saw an increase in its share prices by over 160%.

As most of the dividend-paying stocks do not experience market volatility to a significant degree because of their steady business model and ability to develop cash flow, they are preferred by both beginner and mature investors.

Dividend stocks, on the whole, perform better than other investment sources because of various reasons. These are discussed one by one in the following sections.

Historical Data

It is believed that dividend stocks always serve as a cushion against the unstable business setting. Though previous performance is never indicative of the future prospects, the Standard & Poor's 500-stock index returns have always been outperformed by the dividend stock. From 1960 onwards, dividend stocks provided nearly 29% of the overall returns of the S&P 500. In the past few decades, stocks that pay dividend have consistently been outperforming stocks that do not give dividends, and it is predicted by analysts that the dividend payers will continue this behavior in the long-run.

On the basis of the study RBC Global Asset Management, 11.7% compounded annual returns were generated by dividend stocks in the preceding three decades. It was also determined in the Hartford Funds white paper that almost 81% of S&P 500 returns from 1960 are generated by reinvested dividends due to the compounding factor.

Higher Earnings Quality

Accounting fully revolves around estimates and presumptions. Lately, efforts have being made by various companies and businesses to present false presumptions and estimates. It is very easy for them to do this by making certain modifications in their depreciation techniques. On the whole, it is very easy for the management to report high income figures and estimates instead of the actual values.

Companies generally work on these kinds of behavior to bring about a temporary increase in the share price and confidence level of the traders. To identify these methods, investors and traders should be aware of forensic accounting.

Nonetheless, with respect to dividend-paying firms, there is very low possibility of presenting misrepresentative figures. Investors cannot be misled by the management on real cash. Non-cash items are not included in real cash, which decreases the management's ability to report higher figures than the actual ones. Therefore, real cash can be made by making investments in companies that have a long history of giving dividends and which are consistently increasing their dividend payouts.

Dividend Yields are During Market Break Down

Value investing is capable of offering higher returns to investors when there is an increase in price. Nonetheless, they are also capable of generating high losses for investors when the stock market goes through significant downfalls. In times of economic meltdowns, dividend paying stocks continue to remain stronger than the non-dividend paying stock. In general, the balance sheet of the dividend paying companies is very strong, and they have steady business models to deal with any downfalls in the market. Furthermore, there has always been a steady increase in the share price of the dividend-paying firms.

To understand how market adjusts the value of the companies' performance shareholders, we shall develop a demo portfolio. For this, suppose that $100,000 has been invested by investors in two stocks, which are Berkshire Hathaway and Johnson & Johnson. An amount of $50,000 has been invested in each stock. Furthermore, it is assumed that the investor is not managing the portfolio efficiently.

No dividend has been paid by Berkshire Hathaway since 1960. In contrast, there is an extensive dividend history of Johnson & Johnson, and it has increased its dividends every year for the past three decades. The company even managed to increase its dividends during the 2007/2008 worldwide financial turmoil. Furthermore, the share price of the company remained high despite the prevailing conditions because of its steady balance sheet and cash position.

Now let us consider that there has been a market crash and that stock values decreased by almost 50%. This implies that the value of the portfolio fell from $100,000 to $50,000 in just one day, causing a loss of $50,000 to those who had invested in the two stocks. Though the stock price has decreased, a dividend check is given by JNJ every quarter. In addition, the dividend payout will double. The dividends allow the investors to place a floor beneath the share price and make it stable.

Humans instinctively try to keep those investments in which they receive checks regularly and experience consistent increase in their initial investment as the share price increases. Investors are likely to hold those investments in stocks that provide them powerful resistance against the market fluctuations. Furthermore, steady incomes are quite attractive; the markets are essentially going to experience highly complex business scenarios.

Disciplined in Capital Investing

It is important for dividend-paying companies' management to show a greater degree of discipline when handling their cash. These companies divide their cash flows such that they are able to achieve gradual increase in their sales and earnings, while giving cash returns to investors. If the CEO suddenly comes across two prospective opportunities for acquisition, he needs to choose the option that is more profitable and guarantees increased benefits.

There is a significant effect of dividend on the share price performance of any stock. The share prices specifically increase because of the dividend payments that increase with time. Furthermore, the stock prices of companies that are known to increase dividends at a decent rate are able to withstand the market fluctuations, and their steady business models provide a hedge against market fluctuations.

The possibility of generating a stable flow of income by investing in dividend stocks or keeping the stocks in the long term boosts the share price of these companies. Though it may seem that this causes moderate encouragement, the basic beliefs regarding the organization's income are what affect the shares to the greatest extent. It is vital to comprehend the way stock markets operate to determine how financial specialist perspectives are vigorously influenced by dividends.

CHAPTER 1

YOUR MONEY IS NOT SAFE!

Best Place to Save Your Money

Is the stock market the best place to invest your money? What are the other options that you have to invest your money?

Under the Mattress

It is not a smart option to just save cash and not invest it anywhere. There is always the risk of someone breaking into your house and stealing your money, or that of your house getting burnt. Hence, you need to consider inflation and the impact it will have on your future spending ability.

Savings Account

It was possible to obtain a saving account with an interest rate of 5-6% in 2006-2007. Currently, however, it would be hard for you to even get one over 1%. Though it seems that cash in a savings account is safe, its purchasing power slowly decreases. If there is an average inflation of 3.5% each year, which means that the price of goods and services will increase each year, then your dollar today has a worth of just 96.5 cent the following year.

Majority of the people keep cash in a savings account as they are worried that they may lose money if they invest it. However, your money remains worthless across the years. This is also true for CDs because their interest rates have also decreased.

Mutual Funds

A mutual fund refers to a fund in which money from several investors is collected and invested in various securities like stocks and bonds.

When you purchase shares in a mutual fund, you actually have ownership of a small percentage of the different securities leading to more diversification in your portfolio.

It is clear by now that stocks are the most high-risk form of investment. A financial specialist, i.e. the one who handles a mutual fund, limits that risk by trying to distribute the risk across several securities.

An issue with mutual funds is that they involve different kinds of fees, for example administrative fees, management fees, front-end and back-end load, reinvestment charges, etc.

I always assess the expense ratio, which is the percentage charged by your financial institution every year. These expense ratios can be anywhere between 0.5% to more than 1%.

If your investment capital was worth $100,000 in this mutual fund, and your expense ratio was 0.5%, then your expenses for that year would amount to $500. When your investment increased to $200,000 in a few years, you would pay $1,000 in expenses at the same expense ratio.

This is an expensive trade-off to make because you could have used that $1,000 to invest it in other stocks. Here, you need to remember that when you purchase stocks on your own, you just have to pay a commission fee for buying or selling securities.

Another issue with mutual funds is that you no longer have voting rights. The voting rights are only with the institution or the financial expert that owns the mutual fund.

401K

Majority of the organizations now provide their employees the choice to contribute percentage or fixed dollar amount to their 401k. I am in favor of the 401k; however, when you opt for one at your workplace, the only options you have are the investment plans being offered by the company.

In the present times, the most famous 401k funds are the target-date retirement funds that typically have a year at the end, for example Vanguard Target Retirement 2055. The year signifies the retirement year, which suggests that at the start, the fund may have 70-80% of the portfolio in stocks, but when it approaches the retirement date of 2055, the balance of the portfolio will slowly be adjusted to include more secure investments, such as bonds, while decreasing the share of riskier options like investment in stocks.

Similar to the mutual funds, you need to make payments for the expenses.

CHAPTER 2

BUILDING ACCUMULATION PLAN

After you have determined the size of a nest egg that you need to develop to pay the yearly income you require at retirement, you need to formulate a plan to develop that nest egg.

What Age Do You Hope to Retire?

You first need to decide the number of years till your retirement. This answer will be different for everyone because everyone has different plans for retirement. For instance, if you are planning to retire before the usual age of 65, then you may have lesser number of years left to develop your nest egg as compared to someone who is planning to work till the age of 65. A significant part is also played by your current age regarding the number of years you have left till retirement. An individual who has just started his/her job career will have several years left before retirement to save, as compared to someone who is already very close to retirement.

Therefore, there can be different responses, based on each person's individual situation. However, everyone uses the same calculation to determine the number of years that are left to retirement.

The first thing that you need to determine is your retirement age. Do you plan on continuing to work till the standard age of retirement of 65 years, or are you planning to retire earlier? If you plan to retire early, then at what age? There is also the possibility that you love your work so much that you would like to work till as long as you can. You may think that you can continue to work till 70 years of age, or even older.

When deciding your age of retirement, I would suggest you to aim for a younger age. This would provide you a little room for extension because if you are unable to attain your objectives, you will possibly keep working for a few more years. You also need to aim for a younger age because you do not know what health conditions you may face as you get older. You may love working and want to keep on working till as long as you can, but your body may have different plans for you. There are chances that you do not have the physical strength to work beyond 65 years of age.

Hence, I would suggest your aim should be to retire by 65 years of age or younger than that. After determining your age of retirement, you need to calculate the number of years left till you reach that age.

This calculation is one of simple subtraction. Subtract your current age from your planned age of retirement. For instance, if your aim is to retire by 55 years and you are 30 years at present, then you have 25 years left to establish your nest egg.

Do You Have Current Nest Egg?

Now that we have decided the size of the nest egg you are aiming for and the number of years left to reach this goal, we need to determine the retirement savings (if any) that you have managed to build so far. The answer to this is different for every individual; a younger person would have managed to save very less so far for retirement.

However, if a person is older, it is likely that they have managed to set aside some money for retirement during the years they are employed. But this is often not true as people may come across situations in life that deter them from working towards their goals. If this is the case with you, don't worry as we are now going to guide you how to start working towards your objectives.

What is required at this stage is quite simple; however, for a few people, it may require an extra bit of effort. We need to determine all of your present retirement accounts and add them to attain the worth of your existing nest egg.

You need to make sure that you consider all of your retirement accounts. If you have more than one account, you need to check the money invested in each of those accounts. Sometimes, people distribute their retirement savings in a variety of accounts. You may have many 401k from previous and existing employers. You may have an IRA (individual retirement account) or various IRA's with many brokers. Also, take into account any Roth IRA's that you may have.

After determining all of your existing retirement accounts, you just need to add the total amounts of each of these to obtain the value of your present nest egg. In addition, it is also alright if you do not have any existing retirement savings. You will soon start saving for your retirement as we develop a plan and start working on your aims.

How Much More Retirement Savings Do I Need to Reach My Goal?

After deciding the nest egg required for retirement and determine the amount you have saved up so far for your nest egg, you need to determine how much more you need to save to achieve your objective. After we have decided how much is required to save, we can use this information with the number of years left till retirement to develop your nest egg. We will then use this information to develop an accumulation plan.

You can determine the amount of money you need to save further for your retirement savings by just subtracting the amount you have saved so far from your intended total for nest egg. For instance, if you have decided that your overall nest egg should be worth $800,000 at retirement and you have managed to save $50,000 till now, then you need to save $750,000 more before your retirement (800-50=750).

Putting Accumulation Plan Together

The math has been quite simple till now. You just have to use a little bit of subtraction and addition to determine the money you need to save further to achieve your retirement objectives, and the number of years left for accumulating this amount.

We now need to determine the amount you should be saving every month to achieve your intended nest egg.

You first need to make a rough estimation of the return on investments you will be earning with time.

The experts will usually tell you that you may be able to earn a return of 10 to 12% on average from the stock market.

However, I am more in favor of adopting a conservative approach. I am of the view that when developing your plans, you need to make a conservative overall return estimate of approximately 7-8%. I determine this overall return estimate by calculating that we will earn almost 3 to 4% on our portfolio through dividends, and the remaining return will be generated through the rise in stock market.

I believe that when formulating your retirement plans, you need to use figures conservatively so that there is margin for errors. If you are aiming to achieve a 12% return on your investments so that you are able to attain your retirement objectives, you are less likely to achieve your goals. However, if you take a more conservative approach and only depend on the market to provide you with 7% yearly returns, then you have greater chances of attaining your goals. But you should remember that all of these are just estimates and there is no surety regarding your investment returns, which is why you should show flexibility in your plans.

You can use a savings goal calculator by adding your retirement nest egg amount in the savings goal box. Next, add in the number of years left till your retirement goal date and the amount of nest egg you have managed to save so far. In the expected rate of return box, add 7% or 8% (using the conservative approach). After doing this, the chart beneath the calculators input will tell you the amount of monthly savings required to achieve your objectives.

For instance, if you were planning to save $2,000,000 till retirement, and you started off with $40,000 in your nest egg, with 30 more years to save and an expected return of 7%, according to the calculator, you need to save $1,442 every month till your retirement goal date to achieve your target. If you believe that you will be able to save this amount, then go ahead with this; however, if you believe that it is not possible to save this amount each month, then you need to modify your goals.

Making Realistic Plan

You need to make sure that you have a savings plan that you are highly likely to follow. Hence, you may have to make changes in your plan to achieve a monthly savings amount that is attainable and realistic.

You can modify your plan to help you attain your target in two ways.

First, you need to modify the overall amount of money you want to save till retirement. Decreasing your total nest egg target would mean that you will have less money at retirement.

Secondly, you can change the total number of years left for you to save. It may not be possible for you to retire when you wish to retire. In the previous example, if you feel like you may not be able to save $1,442 every month, but you believe that you can save at least $1,000, then you can adjust the years to increase the number of years left to save to 34. When you do so, you will be able to achieve your target by saving $1,000 every month. However, this means that you will have to work for 4 more years than you wanted to.

I suggest that you should increase the number of years you plan to work till your retirement. As you progress in your work, it is likely that you will start earning more in your career, which will increase the amount you can save each month to enable you to achieve your target earlier.

After experimenting with different figures in the calculator, you would have gained an idea of the amount you need to save each month to attain your retirement targets. Determining the amount you need to save each month is the foremost step in establishing an accumulation plan.

It is possible that a few of you may not be able to get the figures in the calculator help you in achieving your target. You may observe that you cannot increase the number of years to the extent that you are able to attain your objective. There is a high chance that you will not be able to achieve your target. If this happens, you need to plan how to save as much as you can in the number of years left till your retirement. We will discuss in detail what can be done when you are unable to achieve your retirement goal in the subsequent sections of the book. At present, you just need to select an amount that you feel you can save every month, and this will be your existing savings number as we move ahead in our accumulation plan.

CHAPTER 3

WHAT ARE YIELDS?

You often come across the term 'yield' when taking investment decisions. It is important for you to understand this term thoroughly so that you are able to obtain the greatest benefits in your investment career. As you are going to hear this term very often, you should ensure that you are able to make the most of what is offered to you by the yields. After learning about the yields, you can determine the ones you should be selecting.

Looking Ahead

Yields represent the forward face of the earnings that your investment will make in the subsequent years. In essence, they predict how the investment is going to move forward. The yield, or prediction, of every company is distinct and is determined by the shares offered by the company.

When determining the investments you should make, you should ensure that you determine its yield. This will tell you the amount of money you can make and what you can expect to achieve. It is important for you to acknowledge that these are just predictions, and do not depend on what happens with the profits at present. They only represent what could happen in the future. Hence, you should ensure that your investment decision is not solely dependent on yields and what will happen in the future.

Not Behind

Yields do not look behind or what happened with distinct payouts in the past. This is the task of the returns. Returns are not the same as yields as they depend on the information and what has happened earlier. They are founded on the basis of authentic information that makes it easier to manage them. It is difficult for people to comprehend that there are differences between the two. However, the best way is to understand it is by remembering that yields look forward.

Returns Look Behind

Returns inform you about what happened when people made investments in the past and how much money they made from it. However, yields only tell you how much money you will make from the investment instead of what people have made in the past. They do not depend on factual information and are only developed to give you an overview. Predictions are made with experts to ensure that they are doing things in the proper way and providing you an idea of how much money you may be able to make.

Often Higher than Returns

Yields are just predictions and are what is referred to as the 'best-case scenario'. Therefore, they are often significantly greater than the return on investments. Investments should be taken to distinct levels. In addition, the returns are not as high as yields as they are based on actual figures.

When you are thinking about purchasing a stock or investing in a firm, you need to keep this in mind regarding the yields. As yields will always be more than the returns, it would be a better idea to review the returns to obtain a more realistic picture of what the company is going to give you in return for your investments.

One may be tempted to review the yields and consider the best-case scenario. However, yields do not offer a realistic picture at all times. If you believe that you will receive the yield amount every time you receive a payment from the company, you are likely to face disappointment when you receive just the return amount or something close to it.

When you comprehend that yields are greater than returns, you are making sure that you do not get disappointed by the money you actually receive on your investment. The dividend payment may be significantly higher than the regular payment. It should be close to the yield, but you should remember that it is usually not very high, and that the yields are often highly ambitious, which is usually never achieved by the dividend payments.

Yields vs. Returns

There are different avenues for investing in returns and yields. It would not be a good idea to compare them with each other regarding which one is better because they are entirely different things. You should comprehend the difference between the two before deciding to select one for investing in.

Yield

When you look at the potential, the yield is excellent. It helps you comprehend the amount of money you can make in an investment. Though it is a prediction, it does have an element of realism and can even make use of the returns to enable it to be the same as it was in distinct scenarios. In some situations, yields can be very useful for people wishing to do more.

Return

If you want to have a realistic attitude when making investments, it would be best to use the return. The return fully pertains to reality and will tell you what you are most likely to make rather than what you could make. Though one may be disappointed when they consider the return instead of the yield, they actually are able to get a better idea of what they are going to do with the information that they have acquired. In addition, using returns, you can determine the most profitable investment for you so that you can do much more with your dividend investment.

CHAPTER 4

HIGH YIELD INVESTMENTS

There are some other unconventional ways in which you can make investments in dividends, which are investments with high yield, and these are discussed in this chapter. We presented an overview of these in the initial chapters, which include the real estate trusts (REITs), BDCs, or master limited partnerships (MLPs). There are benefits and drawbacks of each of these, and so we will review them and determine whether you should be incorporating them in your investments.

REITS

There are two kinds of real estate investment trust, or REIT. An equity REIT is the more common of these, in which property investments are made. In this kind of investment, money is generated by obtaining rent and selling properties. The other kind of REIT is known as a mortgage REIT, which pertains to making loans, and making profits from the interest paid along with the loan. When shares are bought by dividend investors in a REIT most of the times, they will prefer to invest in an equity REIT.

Usually, equity REIT will hold commercial properties; however, they can also have multi-family properties. You may make investments in different kinds of REITs, for instance, one may invest in office buildings, whereas the other may own industrial or retail properties.

Using a REIT, it becomes quite easy to enter into real estate. The trading of REIT takes place similar to stocks, and they are also comparatively less costly. Share prices are almost $100 per share.

Digital Realty Trust (stock ticker DLR) is a suitable example of this. When we check this on Yahoo Finance, we observe that it is currently trading at $115 per share. The forward dividend yield is at 3.67% and the dividend is $4.32, which is quite appealing. This REIT is quite attractive for investment since it is a digital data center REIT. Hence, they hold facilities that are employed for cloud computing. It is expected that this will be demanded in the forthcoming years.

Welltower is a REIT based on healthcare that invests in various entities from hospitals to old-age homes (stock ticker WELL). It has a share price of $82, a yield of 4.67% and a dividend payment of $3.48 for each share.

It can be seen that the dividend payments of REITs are quite high. It may be a better option to invest in DLR instead of Apple if you wish to achieve a higher income level. The cost of DLR per share is lower; hence, there is lower barrier to entry. However, it still gives back almost $2 more than the dividend being paid by Apple.

There are REITs for almost all kinds of properties. For example, Gladstone (LAND) buys and then rents out farmland. AMH (American Homes 4 Rent) is an REIT that buys single-family homes and then rents them out. The price of this REIT is $24/share. This REIT offers low yield and dividend ((0.83% and $0.26, respectively); hence, you may not want to invest in it at present. However, it is mentioned here to show that there are several alternatives for investing in REITs. There are some REITs that own even such unheard items like cell phone towers.

Real estate is possibly one thing that almost everyone has discussed investing in at some point or the other. Nonetheless, if you decided to invest in real estate, you may need to acquire loans or spend a significant amount of money. We shall perform a comparison between REIT investment and purchasing a house for renting it out.

Let us first examine renting a house. Consider, for example, that you purchased a house for $250,000, in Denver, Salt Lake City or Colorado. We choose a mid-sized to a large Western city to not have to worry about the extremely high rent prices in cities like San Francisco, New York City or Los Angeles. The ideal scenario is one where you pay cash. A home bought at this price may be able to fetch a rent of approximately $1,400 per month. Apart from this, there are property taxes; however, we will assume that the additional expenses are covered by the tenant. After considering the property taxes and other incidental experiences, which are not very high in western cities, we can assume that you will be able to make a profit of $1,100 a month. In this price, you will be able to cover up your cost of $250,000 in 228 months, which is almost 19 years. This means that during this time, you have not made any profit.

If you make a down payment of $25,000 and obtain a loan for the remaining, a mortgage of 15 years would incur a cost of $1,655 per month. This may not cut down your market so you may take the benefit of the difference in the rent that was being paid, or you could go for a typical 30-year mortgage. In this situation, when the interest is 3.92%, you would receive a mortgage payment of $1,092. Hence, you are essentially breaking even, but the mortgage is being paid by the tenant.

However, if you decide to invest $250,000 in DLR, you will receive dividend payments of almost $8,700 on an annual basis. Through the $250,000 gets locked in the investment, no mortgage payment is to be made. If required, you may reinvest the money from dividends and buy 75 or more shares each year and benefit from compound interest to increase your principal with the passage of time.

Here, it may all be about your preference, but REITs permit you to enter into the property business without actually having to own properties. To actually make investments in real estate, you can purchase some houses if you have the money or the credit for it. However, you will have to work with tenants, pay for the maintenance of the properties, renovate the house from time to time or at least set up new flooring and change bathrooms. This is not as simple as it seems. Using REIT investments, you can gain access to different kinds of real estate, while all the hassles are managed by other people. In addition, getting out of this market is quite simple as you just need to place a sell order with your broker.

REITs are those institutions that do not pay corporate taxes and divide majority of their earnings among the shareholders.

They usually payout about 90% of their earnings. Before you purchase an REIT, you may want to find out more information about it in the same way as you would before you invest in a company. You may want to determine how their income is generated. You will look for Fund from Operations with REITs, which is also written as FFO. FFO is computed using net income, interest income, depreciation and gains or losses from selling properties. There will also be an adjusted FFO of REIT, which modifies the FFO by considering a few other items that are subtracted from the FFO computation. These may consist of money required for the maintenance of properties, unrealized gains and rent.

A few REITs may compute their FFO using a different method than others; however, you can employ the ratio of share price to FFO. A high FFO value is more profitable.

Just like stocks, you may have to view the performance with time, specifically their cash flow. You will also view their yield and dividend payouts to determine if it belongs to the range of dividend payments that you are looking for. If the growth rate of FFO remains good over a period of many years, then it is a good REIT option for investment.

Similar to any other form of investment in the present times, an exchange-traded fund can be used for investment in REITs. There are many benefits of this. Firstly, it offers diversity in the kinds of exposure. This means that rather than purchasing a single REIT yourself that concentrates on one kind of property, you can opt for an ETF that has invested in hundreds of REITs. They will made investments in different kinds of REITs, which means that you will be exposed to different areas, such as hospitals, home rentals, land, digital, etc.

IYR is a real estate REIT ETF offered by iShares. It makes investments in companies that are listed on the Dow Jones Real Estate Investment Index. Vanguard VNQ is another well-known and well-established REIT ETF. You can check their websites to determine their past performance. It is asserted by iShares that if you had made investments worth $10,000 in IYR 20 years ago, you would have earned $50,000 in equity so far. This, however, does not consider the money earned (and which has likely been reinvested) from dividends.

REITs can turn out to be an interesting investment that should be incorporated in your portfolio. However, you should be aware that they do have certain risks, the greatest of which is the interest rate risk. As they are part of real estate, several loans may be taken by REITs. When interest rates are high, it may mean that the REIT may incur greater expenses. However, other factors need to be taken into account. For example, the situation of the higher rate of interest and the events taking place in the overall economy. Based on the situation, higher rates of interest may signify increased profits for REIT. Whatever the situation is, an REIT should be considered as a long-term investment. Therefore, the typical buy-and-hold strategy is applicable here, unless you have other strong reasons to invest somewhere else.

MLP

We now consider MLPs, which refer to master limited partnerships. As asserted in the first chapter, this is a partnership business that is traded publicly as a stock. The trading of MLPs takes place on the key exchanges. However, it functions as a partnership, hence, when investors get their share, tax will be imposed on the profits. An MLP is needed to distribute the cash available among investors. It involves general partners and limited partners. Being an investor, you will be considered as a limited partner as you are not at all involved in the routine tasks of an MLP.

According to the law, an MLP has to distribute 90% of its earnings to its investors. MLPS were restrained by Congress to a few sectors as they were disappointed that corporate income taxes are not being paid by MLPS, and are still being traded publicly. Hence, MLPs are restricted to real estate, finance and energy sectors. As majority of the real estate operators are REITs, most of the MLPs belong to the energy sector. Oil and gas operations are part of MLPs. This is typical for a transportation or infrastructure company, which will carry out the distribution of oil, oil pipelines or oil refinement facilities. They do not show high sensitivity to oil and gas prices like a direct energy company such as Exxon since they are paid by the volume of oil or gas they are able to transmit.

An MLP provides a tax benefit to the investor, which indicates that it enables them to balance their tax bill to a large extent. As the investor, you have to bear depreciation and depletion costs, and you include these in your own taxes, which can lead to significant amounts of tax savings. This happens because being a partner, you have a share in the company assets, and so, you are able to use depreciation to your advantage. You should note that if you make investments in an MLP ETF, these tax benefits are not applicable to you.

Though you should possibly avoid investing in an MLP ETF, investing in MLPs is simple because their trading is carried out in the same way as the normal stocks on major exchanges. They work as dividend stocks; however, the income distributed from MLPs is known as distribution instead of a dividend, and is paid on a quarterly basis. For tax purposes, this income is considered as a return on capital. This suggests that tax is not imposed on most of your distributions from the MLP till you sell your shares (units). You could avert taxes by not selling, or you can sell them and pay capital gains taxes. Yields from MLPs are usually quite attractive.

For instance, Enterprise Product Partners (EPD) that owns oil pipelines provides a yield of 6.11% and a distribution of $1.75 (paid on a quarterly basis, yearly amount). The price per unit share is almost $25. The trading price of Magellan midstream partners (MMP) is $62, providing a yield of 6.54% and a distribution of $4.02. "Midstream" is the term used for a company that transmits energy, while "upstream" refers to the ones carrying out the actual drilling.

You lose the tax benefits if you purchase an MLP ETF, which means that it would be better to just invest in the MLPs. We can be sure of the fact that energy is not going to end so soon, even if it is believed by Alexandira Ocasio Cortez that it will be fully changed in 12 years. It is likely that she is wrong about this and that these are actually suitable investments.

You would want to perform an analysis of the financials of any MLP that you are seeking to invest in. Interest consists of three items. The first pertains to the amount of cash that is paid by the MLP to the partners (i.e. investors). The second is the DCF that is paid by the DCF (Distributable Cash Flow). This essentially refers to the cash left over after expenses are deducted and the general partner is paid. This will consist of depreciation, net income and capital expenses such as maintenance of the pipelines or establishing new ones.

After you have determined DCF, you will also want to determine the coverage ratio or CR, which is DCF, divided by the cash divided among the unit-holders. This informs how the health of the MLP is in terms of making cash payments to unit-holders. When the coverage ratio is lower than 1.0, it suggests that the MLP was unable to pay the shareholders. Hence, you may want to avoid this MLP. You should look at the coverage ratio before investing.

As you are not going to use an ETF due to its tax effects, when seeking to invest in MLPs, you should manage your own diversification. It would be a good idea to invest in around 5 to 10 MLPs. Choose MLPs that provide high yields and coverage ratios more than 1.0.

BDCs

Business Development Company, BDC, is an investment company that usually makes investments in small to mid-sized companies. BDCs usually target the companies that are in their initial stages and require funds to grow. These companies cannot usually obtain funds from other places.

The BDC was established by the Congress in 1980 as a structure. If the company successfully fulfills specific requirements that have been established by the law, for example distributing the least required amount of cash flow among the investors, it can be considered as a BDC and no longer pay corporate income taxes. Hence, a BDC typically functions as a company that passes on its income to investors. A few of these pass on up to 98% of their income, which can be considered as extremely high yields.

BDCs can actually function as venture capital firms that invest cash for equity in small and medium-sized businesses that are developing. A BDC can also give loans to other companies. The BDC also functions as a salvage operation at times by investing in or giving loans to a business that is currently facing money shortages so as to help it come out of its troubles.

The yields for BDCs are usually in the range of 8 to 12%.

Saratoga Investment Corporation (ticker SAR) is a BDC that offers investment capital to help companies facing problems. The company can offer investments amounting to $20 million

Secured loans are offered by several BDCs to small and medium-sized businesses. Apollo Investment Corp (AINV) is one company that does so. This kind of company is said to offer a solid investment. As it gives loans, it continues to get a stable source of income as interest.

CHAPTER 5

USING DIVIDENDS AS PASSIVE INCOME

A bear market is observed to happen every 3.5 years. This means that in 118 years, as Ned Davis calculated, a bear market has come about 32 times and at an average; each bear market may extend over a period of 15 months, finds Azaad Asset Management. This period sees a plunge in stock prices by more than 30%. To put into perspective, a 17-month long bear market has been recently recorded. How does studying these statistics benefit us? Sometimes market crashes and bear markets are inevitable and investors obviously suffer the loss. But believe it or not, the stock markets have some investors who remain unaffected through such variations. They achieve this by investing in dividends. Hence, regardless of the market situation, the investor reaps dividends every month or every year. This advantage gains dividends the rank of one of the best sources of passive income. Dividend investment is one of the most flexible, yet stable sources of incomes in the market not only for people approaching the age of retirement, but also for people who are looking into side investments along with their primary occupations. This form of investment guarantees returns whilst maintaining the capital investment. This means that the benefits of purchasing investment stocks include a steady/regular income as the value of the stock improves in the market. Moving into this subject, we will probe the fundamentals of dividend investments and suggest implementable methods to use it to our advantage.

Misconceptions of Dividend Investment

Earlier in this topic, the context revolved around the word "Dream". We all dream and work towards perfecting our lives, enjoying vacations, a roof over the head, owning one of the best cars- the list is endless. These dreams serve as a guiding and driving force for our ambitions. Your desire to fulfill your dreams may even have led you to read this book. There are certain theories about dividends which are slightly overrated and may lead to false hopes and below we will explain the reality of dividends and how to make the best of it.

High Yields Are Priority

Many investors base their investments on little research and instinctively invest in stocks with high paying returns. On the contrary, this may not always be as lucrative as one may think. Stocks with higher rates of return can sometimes be an irresistible bait so as to lure investments. We can understand this better by studying some of the stocks that pay every month. One must understand that higher rates of dividends do not directly imply that the company must be performing well. How do we infer this? Corus Entertainment paid high amounts of dividends at the rate of 26.9 percent during the third quarter of 2018.

When we study this company's returns and investments in detail, we find that the company is not increasing its capital by reinvesting, rather it is paying out larger portions of the profit into dividends, diminishing its capacity to grow. Corus Entertainment holds a −18.54% annualized accumulative return over a period of three years and a −1.81% annualized accumulative return over a period of ten years. Companies that are incapable of expansion are slowly but surely eliminated from the market over a course of time. To top it off, investing in such companies is unavoidable to some extent if we observe the ratio of dividend payout since this ratio represents the percentage of profits that the shareholders receive.

With that being said, several stock market sectors have a high rate of recompense because it is embedded in their corporate structure. These sectors primarily include real estate trusts and master limited partnerships. The corporate structure of these sectors is such that it allows for high dividend generation and payout ratios.

Dividends Guarantee Downside Protection and Upside Potentials

Several fallacies also surround the concept of dividend income. Strong advocates of stock dividends exaggerate the benefits of investing in them. Many have stated that the market price depreciation that occurs during economic recessions can be countered with the help dividends. We find this to be exaggerated because "Dividends just offer a little shock absorption against crashing stock prices".

Dividend investments can make for a successful source of income if expectations are realistic and reasonable. Aspects to be considered while investing in certain stocks should be dividend generation as well as overall returns. Not only this, one should also consider newly introduced companies that seem to be making a name. Playing too safe can also not be fruitful for the investors. This means that one should not limit his market research to companies that have been around for more than two decades and paying their dividends diligently but also invest in new ones that are performing efficiently.

Why Is Dividend Investment So Powerful?

Realistically, we rarely find two people engaged in a conversation about dividend investment. It isn't everyone's cup of tea when it comes to talking finances. Comparing to other options on the table, the currently trending tech stocks like that of Amazon, Netflix, Facebook etc. tend to sideline the greater good of dividends i.e. the impact of compound interest. In a nutshell, compound interest is the cumulative interest that you receive on the capital and the interest that you don't withdraw. Basically, one keeps expanding their capital and hence the interest also increases. To put in perspective, consider an investment in Coca-Cola stock dividends. Say you invested $10,000 in 1962 and kept reinvesting your received dividends into the same company till 2012, nearly 50 years later. Your receivable investment now would be a jaw dropping $2 million.

Dividends are not only a source of generating passive income, but in times of inflation, it saves a volatile market from nose diving into losses. Dividends are found to be increased by 4.2% since 1912 against an augmented inflation of 3.3%. The math here is simple and it implies that our investments are safe. Furthermore, the fall of stock market often increases the dividend generation

Why Do Companies Pay Dividends?

So far, our discussion has been about the obvious, that dividends are an effective source of passive income. Our discussion regarding "dividend investments" is far broader than this. You would be surprised to know that dividend paying companies facilitate their investors with certain tax benefits as well, which we all would happily accept. But putting all of these pros aside, we shall shed some light on why some companies pay dividends and others choose not to. We will probe further into the theories that support dividend investments and then those which are against it, then study the policies that every company considers before calculating the dividend recompenses.

Arguments against Dividends

The status of dividend investment is one of the most under-rated categories amongst other methods of investment. Even though their annual net-worth is substantial, tech corporation tycoons like Amazon, Facebook etc. are not in the favor of paying dividends. Not only these companies, but also market big shots like Berkshire Hathaway which is the Holding company owned by billionaire and investor Warren Buffet does not believe in becoming a dividend paying company. You will find several successful investors also who will advise against investing in dividends to generate income from the stock market.

The global and technical equity strategist, Sameer Sama working for Wells Fargo Investment Institute in St Louis states that "Investors become habitual to receive dividends from dividend-paying companies which then becomes binding on the company to pay it in any case and the company is under pressure when it tries to cut down or stop paying dividends, hence companies like to pay special dividends which offer flexibility of withdrawal"."

Sameer Sana is also of the opinion that an investor can benefit from the trend of little to no dividend returns. He based this argument on the observation that heavier taxes are levied upon the dividends as compared to capital gains. He further suggests that a better choice for companies looking to expand their value in the stock market is to reinvest their profits and increasing their capital so as to raise their stock value. The advocates of this notion suggest that instead of distributing a portion of their profits in the form of dividends, a company should look into expansion options like re-investing in financial assets, acquiring new assets, and re-purchasing the company's own shares.

Arguments for Dividends

Now while the above argument may be uninspiring and enough to put off any potential investor, we should also study the companies that prefer paying dividends. Some arguments stated in this section are sufficient to counter the arguments against it, especially that paying dividends inhibits the company's capacity to expand. If we observe 2 prime corporations namely the 3M Co and Johnson and Johnson, we will understand this better. For over 60 years now, 3M Co. (MMM) has been indemnifying its investors with dividends. Since 2012, the dividend per share has doubled to $4.70. Also, since President Kennedy's time, Johnson and Johnson have been paying its investors dividends, today each of their shares sells at $125. Their product quality and variety, both have improved since they commenced and stocks have risen by 45% since last half a decade.

How does this serve the company in the long run? This practice of paying dividends upon shares assures the investor about financial standing of the company. Therefore, old-school companies and companies with a strong trustful position amongst the customer make it a tradition to pay dividends to their investors as per the sayings that the ability to pay out dividends is often correlated with a sound financial standing of the company by the investors. This reflects well on the company stocks as well when the investors are paid their due dividends.

CHAPTER 6

BUYING DIVIDEND PAYING STOCKS

If the above information has convinced you enough to invest in dividend paying stocks, then you should be considering methods to purchase them. Purchasing individual stocks is not much different from buying stocks. One can do so by involving a broker in the process or approach the company. The benefits of involving a broker in the process is acquiring an opinion, second to your own research so as to decide on investing the best options in the market.

An investor must be aware that there are better choices of investment for acquiring dividend paying stocks rather than investing in individual stocks. An investor may choose a mutual fund to invest in which can have multiple advantages for the investor. One major advantage being that the investor is able to invest in a range of shares which allows him to diversify his portfolio and divide his risk across various stocks. This method also enables the investor to minimize the broker fee.

Buying and Managing Your Dividend Portfolio

When it comes to stock investment, one shouldn't put all their eggs in one basket. If an investor aims to create their portfolio, their chances are improved by investing in more than one kind of stocks. This means that the risks are divided and the portfolio will not remain stagnant for extended periods. One may question the requirement of building a portfolio. To add weightage to one's portfolio, one has to look beyond the quantity of stocks owned to enjoy its true benefits.

Once an investor gains experience of various kinds of stocks, they choose the sector that they want to pursue and reflect in their portfolios. The choice of stocks should be what one finds best and benefits that one should seek from this should be of the long run, rather than the short run benefits.

For establishing a stock dividend portfolio, the following critical aspects should be kept in mind:

Goals: dividend investment shouldn't be based on fluke investments and due consideration should be given to what one aims to acquire through these investments. While all dividend investments make for an easy source of passive income and with wise handling of finances, one can build wealth in the long run, yet not all portfolios serve the investor in the same manner. Your portfolio should not be similar to what the majority are engaging in and this should be based on what your ambitions in life are. Consider the following things to understand what you want to achieve:

- What kind of yield are you targeting?
- How much risk can you take?
- Past experiences of investment
- How long can you keep your investments bound in dividend?
- Time you can spare to learn more about stocks.

Targeting Returns: Once you figure out your ambitions, the next aspect to take into consideration is the average portfolio dividend yield. Every time the dividend is received by you, it should meet the expectations of your average returns and they should also be comparable to the investments that you have made. Suppose the income from dividends is meant to serve for your basic necessities, then consider investing in stocks that will yield higher returns. On the contrary, if you intend to enjoy the returns after several years, then your concern will more be about the growth of dividends and how big the sum of dividends is.

Analyze your Strengths: we all have our strengths and our weaknesses, even when we consider careers. As an investor, through all the trials and errors, one should analyze and work on fortes that are their strengths. There are fortes that become your strengths and then there are other fortes in which investors invest comfortably. The fewer sectors that you invest in, the higher are your chances of loss. This is because if that particular sector faces a recession period, an investor could end up losing a lot of money. Hence the contingency plan is to invest in several sectors. The income may not be the same but it's a safer in times of crises since some sectors can be affected more than the others.

Social Responsibility over Income: some companies may be involved in practices that may be either illegal or unethical in some ways while they may be paying high dividends. As an investor, one should always invest in stocks of companies which practice transparency in their work. For the sake of expanding a portfolio, one should not overlook their responsibility towards the society. These should become one's principles and ethics when deciding to invest. To help you through this, we would suggest in deciding a set of standards that your potential investment company should fall upon. This way, one will rest assured that their money is not being used in illegal practices.

Remain aloof with Relevant Information: once you have decided on your niche for the portfolio, you may begin to build it. Luckily it is the age of internet and information is available at our finger tips hence facilitating us in making choices regarding the kind of stocks we would like on our portfolio. One recommended platform for this is Yahoo Finance to search for the most trending and successful companies to invest in. If you are a beginner at this, you may also find certain apps and websites that will simplify the list of high performing stocks to make the choice easier. Learn to tackle the internet to your advantage and refine your profile to be better than before.

Small Steps towards Making it Big: investing all your money in the stocks all together is not a very wise way to go about it. Once you have decided on what companies you want to invest in, your action should be steady and well thought out. Investments are either mindless or mindful contrary to the saying that a successful investor does not risk it all and takes steady and wise decisions of investments. One must understand that all good things take time and this is no different. The first few investments should be smaller so as to test the waters and over time this should be invested into accordingly. Make it a practice to average your buying price over a certain period of time, this way you will be able to realize if you are making profit in the process or not.

Expand the Big Potential: we recommend starting small so that one can observe the market situation and familiarize themselves with companies of interest. Through this process you should be able to recognize which investments are profitable and which keep you either stagnant or grow slowly. Your portfolio should have the flexibility to withstand pressures of the market and one needs to keep a keen eye for such stocks. There are some companies which are less volatile to market fluctuations. Your target should be to identify those and concentrate on investing in those. However, do not withdraw from small companies altogether, since a small amount of investment in those will allow you to become familiar with them and contribute to your learning process.

CHAPTER 7

FUNDAMENTAL ANALYSIS AND STRATEGIES

Every dividend stock portfolio can benefit from fundamental analysis for optimizing profits and eliminating risks. Comparing it to technical analysis, we find that fundamental analysis is simpler and more doable. An investor can optimize their profits if they have a grasp over the dynamics of the industry. That way, they will be prepared to counter any risks that come their way. This is crucial for any investor who is analyzing the fundamentals of any organization; basic familiarity of that industry in general can be played to their benefit. The best returns are generated if and when the investor understands how the company or that particular industry works.

Consider Caterpillar (CAT) for example. CAT is one of the biggest manufacturers of heavy machinery. In the past two years, this company underwent extreme volatile market situations. Yet the investors who understand the tricks of the market movement and the manufacturing industry and those who know the position of CAT as a company have continued to receive substantial profits due to the volatility of CAT's price.

Between 2013 and mid of 2015, a single share was being traded for $90 and $110. But the second half of the year 2015 brought it to the lowest it has ever been and beginning the FY2016 at $59 a share. Investors who had done their due fundamental analysis did not panic during this time and did not withdraw their investments. The downfall was credited to their short-term fundamentals which are mostly unprotected against external circumstances. The company is related with an industry which operates on all things energy, agriculture and infrastructure etc. Hence the mere fluctuation in the commodity prices can affect its activities. However, this effect is short lived and mostly recoverable.

Commodity prices saw a hike in 2016. In turn the companies that utilize CAT's machinery and relevant products reduced their demand and hence the business did not flourish as usual. The share prices also started to go down. The second half of 2016 however, brought in demand from the end market proving well for the stock market. The CAT share price has come a long way since 2016 and currently stands at a substantially higher rate i.e. $140 a share.

Caterpillar, as a company, checks all the boxes for an investor's portfolio. It offers low payout ratio, high dividend generation, an elaborate history of dividends and a capacity to augment the cashflow. In the situation described above, potential investors could have generated more than 118% profit in comparison to the price that they would have bought it on.

The company maintains a management that is favorable to the shareholders enabling it to withstand the 2016 crisis. Not only that, but it has maintained and improved the tradition of paying dividends.

With that being said, a company should not always be invested into during a time of decline. Besides the ideal opportunity to invest, an investor should also take a look in to other aspects of the company and the fundamental metrics to decide the worthiness of the company. Things to be taken into consideration are discussed below.

Consider Companies with Long Histories

Companies with elaborate histories of being functional are a choice of Buffett, like American Express, Wells Fargo and Coca-Cola are companies established in the 1800s, they continue to flourish and their history dates back to over a century.

One reason an investor should opt for companies with elaborate histories is that there is nothing they haven't seen through time. Over the years, they have established policies to suit their requirements and circumstances, a big record of balance sheets to refer to and the fact that it survived through rough times and through business and technological innovations makes them an ideal choice. For a business to evolve as the times evolve, it needs to constantly evolve its policies and methodologies. Functioning in an industry where innovations are not rapid is also favorable for the business.

The choice of functioning in an industry in which innovations are not rapid enables a company to retain its finances as profits rather than investing them constantly in growth opportunities to keep up with the market pace. If we observe Buffett's favorite five investment companies, we see that only one of them is in an industry where innovations and evolution of the market is rapid, the other four belong to industries that enjoy steady innovations. Companies with extended histories are able to withstand these risks and can generate long-term benefits.

Company Must Have Strong Competitive Advantage

The strength of a company is also the recognition that the brand holds in the market. Investors, especially ones new in the field invest in stocks that are most popular. This requires the company to be capable to expand and evolve as the market trends. Over a long-run, this ability can facilitate the organization to increase its capital from the market shares.

To understand competitive advantage, Blackberry (BBRY) is a good example of a company that lost market standing due to lack of evolution that is comparable to the competitors. The share prices of

Blackberry plunged from $200 down to $10 a share and the market that once belonged to Blackberry, was then owned by Samsung, Apple and numerous other Android phones.

The ability of a company to survive in the long-run over rapid innovations should be one critical aspect to be considered by long-term investors. Consider the technology industry for example. Its market is constantly evolving for two reasons, 1) to become better than before and 2) due to the competition in the industry. Regardless of these challenges, Microsoft (MSFT) thrives in the market and is keeping up with the market trends of evolution.

Make Long Run Strategy

If an investor has time and patience to invest in a company for a long-term, the durability of the company must be assessed before one invests. To gain optimum profits from dividend returns, an investor should be ready to invest for a longer time period.

Investing your time and money in durable companies has many benefits for the investor. Goes without saying, that long-term benefits of a good company will reflect in due time and the returns will be evident over the period of time.

We can consider Coca-Cola to understand the significance of long-term strategies. Coca-Cola is one such dividend mogul which has yielded increasing dividends to its investors and has enjoyed a rise in its share prices over the long-run, proving the benefits of holding stocks over long-run.

Companies with stable business models prove to be a good option for compounding. Such companies are sure to bring substantial amounts of returns to the investors. Furthermore, the tax benefits that come with long-term benefits are also noticeable since every time one sells stocks, taxes are levied upon the seller. Investors often choose not to sell their investments for a longer period and by choosing to do so, the investor is retaining the money that would otherwise be spent in capital charges.

Furthermore, the portfolio turnover of an investor becomes reduced as they make several short-term investments. Maintaining a low prediction cost would demand more investments and the frictional costs will also be reduced by lowering the portfolio turnover. Frictional costs include aspects like slippage, financier exchange costs etc.

Do Fundamental Analysis to find Undervalued Businesses

Benjamin Graham suggested investing in companies that are functioning below their due value in the market. This way when they reach their full potential in the course of time, the investor will enjoy good profits. This method of investment is advocated by many when choosing a suitable company for investments.

Circumstances should also be considered when considering a company for investments. Sometimes losses are subject to temporary circumstances and good companies often bounce back. An investor can choose to invest in stocks that are usually on the higher side, but temporarily suffer losses. In contrast, over-valued stocks should also be avoided as these rises are also short-lived.

The question is about how do we recognize companies that are functioning below their fair value? The easiest of many ways, is to study the ratio of price to earnings to realize the price of the stock's share. Low price trading stocks to earnings ratio should be the focal point of the investor.

Besides this, quality stocks should also be the preference of the investors. Many quality stocks are dismissed by the investors due to poor and temporary circumstances of the economy. For example, McDonald's suffered low stock prices given their restructuring measures and BP stocks suffered a downfall post an oil-spill event. Both companies have come back stronger and thrived since the past two years.

Look for Shareholder Friendly Management

A shareholder friendly company will ensure that the investor benefits from investing in their company. The jurisdiction of how the profits are to be distributed and utilized remains with the management. This means that they decide when and how much of the profits will be distributed to the investors. Older companies with good dividend histories tend to give 30%-50% of their profits in the form of dividends and retain and capitalize the remaining in the company.

A shareholder friendly company will ensure that this practice is maintained and conducted smoothly. Phillip Morris is a good example of a company that retains some portion of the profits and distributes dividends from the other portion. Their dividend history is extensive and the management ensures that dividends are either paid or the investors are given the option of share buybacks. This practice does not hinder their future growth either.

The management at Phillip Morris maintains the dividend yield at 5% and they acknowledge the significance of it. The company has worked on reducing its financial liabilities by reducing the number of outstanding shares. They did this by increasing their funds with the help of financial markets along with their own cash generated. By doing so, they did not have to pay dividends to the fewer shareholders and benefitted them by augmenting the value of every share.

Dividend Payout Ratio

The coverage ratio of the dividends is a method of gauging their safety and this should be top priority of every investor when choosing a dividend stock for the profile. The payout ratio of stocks that the investor should prioritize is 30%-50%. To put in perspective, a company can pay up to $30million to $50 million if the profit of the company is $100 million. Furthermore, such companies ensure that their policies are made to augment profits and revenues which are durable. This is beneficial for the investor since the payout ratio analysis will assure them of higher dividends with every passing year.

A payout ratio of 90% is also maintained by some companies. As good as it may sound, this means that the company is not warranted against crises situations of the market. So, if the market situation makes a company suffer losses of 10%-20% then the company will not be able to distribute the 90% of the dividends and earn a bad name too. U.S. energy companies are one such example in which the payout ratio was high and then had to be slashed by 60% or more after the oil prices dropped in 2016.

Focus on Straight Forward Approach, Either High Dividend Yield or High Dividend Growth Rate Approach

Dividend safety needs to be checked after which the investors select if they want high dividend yield stocks or high dividend growth stocks. Every portfolio has its own set of followers based on what their preferences are. A high dividend yield of a business implies that the business model of the particular organization is stable and that they maintain discipline in their capital growth so as to keep everything moving steadily. In contrast, it is critical for companies that yield higher dividend growths, to generate higher incomes so that they can meet their profit requirements, as well as distribute their due dividends.

CHAPTER 8

HOW TO UNDERSTAND DIFFERENT TYPES OF CANDLESTICKS?

There are several charting platforms out there, one of them is trading view which is currently the most popular among the rest and is a good choice for beginners. Once you have entered the website, go to the center of the screen on the home page and select Launch Chart tab. This will take you to the AAPL page, which is the symbol for **Apple.**

If you wish to switch to another stock select the AAPL ticker on the top-left corner of your screen. Once it is highlighted, type in the symbol of the stock you desire to view and you will get a list of relevant options to choose from.

The website will lead you to a page with a candlestick chart on it, irrespective of your choice of stock ticker. The price action is represented by the candlesticks that take up the majority of the screen.

The volume of shares being traded is shown under the price action candlesticks in the form bars. We cannot disregard the importance of volume in trading. However, in this chapter, we will discuss the price action candlesticks primarily.

How to Know Price Range of Trading Period?

If you look at the candlestick chart closely, you will observe that each candle is different from the other, with some of them having longer lower wicks and others with longer upper wicks. When the lower wick has approached a price point of $9.75, and upper wick has arrived the price point of $10.25, then we say that $9.75 to $10.25 was the price point for the time being observed.

The time frame on the trading view website is 'Daily Chart' as a default setting. If you wish to change this to meet your convenience, go to the top-left corner your screen and select the symbol D. a list of available options will appear as a drop-down list where you can select your desired time frame.

Your trading type decides the time-frame that you must consider. For example, a day trader prefers to view the activity in the same day. On the other hand, a swing trader "swings" from one position to another quickly and might stay on that position for an extended time. Staying on one position for an extended time or over months makes one a long-term investor.

A day trader is expected to overview the daily charts, and vigilantly view the 1 minute and 5minute charts. A swing trader will make use of the 4-hour, daily and weekly charts. A monthly chart will be the strength of a long-term investor for making his investment decisions.

The trading methods that you choose, depends on what method becomes your strength. Many investors prefer to maintain day-trading positions because they are not willing to risk the investments in-case of crises hitting suddenly. News regarding the trading sessions could impact the activity of the stocks therefore many news sources post news regarding trades after the markets close to prevent sudden breakdown of the stock market.

I experimented with day-trading and swing trading to see which method was more profitable. I observed that the profit/loss ratio of both the methods is mostly the same, and we cannot establish the superiority of one method over the other.

How to Know Where Opening and Closing of Time Frame Is?

You can get to know the opening and closing of the candlestick through its color.

A red candlestick shows that the solid candle body's top is where the time frame opened.

Note: With that being said, it should be noted that a wick is not part of a solid candle body. If there's a wick, you can be sure that the price kept on changing from that specific position. In cases that involve a daily chart with a candlestick having a wick at $5 but the topmost point of the solid candle body is at $4, it is being shown that it has only been a few hours at max since price trading was occurring at 5$, which later decremented with 4$ as its closing point. With these conditions, 5$ was the candle's high, which did not last long and fall down to $4, thus forming a wick.

For the red candle, the solid candle body's bottom is where the time frame gets closed.

The reverse is true when the candlestick is green. This means that the solid candle body's bottom and top are where the time frame opens and closes, respectively.

Here's a piece of advice: You can skip green and red and go with white and black candlestick charts since the chart looks boring this way which is beneficial as explained subsequently.

In the world of trading, you are more likely to progress if you're getting bored in comparison to when you're excited or worried. So, instead of going with brighter colors like red or green, you can opt for black and white charts which suppress the emotions of excitement and worry, thus beneficial for the trader.

If you're able to push your emotions to the side, you'll be less likely to make decisions driven by them, which could cause you a loss. For people who feel like they get all hyped up by seeing green candles or start panicking upon getting red candles, you're better off working with the white and black candlestick chart.

Candlestick Names and Definitions

First of all, it's good to briefly explain a few common candlesticks that you'll be seeing on stock charts:

DOJI: When you see an inverted cross, cross, or plus sign, best believe that it's a doji, which is a wick that's appears quite prominent on the candle body.

DRAGONFLY DOJI: If you see a T-shaped wick at the top of the candlestick, you can start referring to as dragonfly doji.

GRAVESTONE DOJI: Get the letter 'T' upside down and you'll have this candlestick.

LONG BODY/LONG DAY: It's this candlestick if it has a long body that's mostly solid with a small wick on its two ends.

LONG SHADOW: The only thing that distinguishes this from a doji is that it's more solid.

MARUBOZU: If it's a solid candle with no wick, then it's this one.

SPINNING TOP: This is the candlestick if it's a small candle toward the wick's center and seems similar to a spinning top.

CHAPTER 9

PICK STOCKS FOR APPRECIATION

Appreciation is not possible for the majority of stock having poor basics. With that being said, we present the following cases where things were a bit different:

- A new product
- A new drug is tested positive
- Acquisition
- Settlement of a legal dispute
- A new advancement or discovery

Firstly, the stocks have to be screened. Afterward, they have to be individually analyzed.

The website of the company, Q10, and the Earning Conference Call are the best sources of updated information, while SeekingAlpha is the easier hub. In comparison to a great percentage of other websites apart from the aforementioned one, it can be seen that Finviz.com provides the latest info.

Although this topic is also concerned with the best time of selling the stock, there are differing concepts/techniques.

With the help of the better analysis, you will be able to get the chances of succeeding.

Quick Fundamental Analysis

Thus far, research has been done on a lot of stocks with the majority of them freely available to the general public. As my starting point, there are five free sites found in the link, which I will give a score to later on. Fidelity customers are suggested to give a shot to their Analyst Opinions.

Several Sources

Zacks, The Street, Value Line, and Morningstar at the top of the list. You should head to your library if you can't find them online for free.

A Simple Scoring System

Open Finviz.com and input the stock symbol afterward.

No.	Metric	Good	Bad	Score
1	Forward P/E1	Between 2.5 and 12.5, Score = 2	> 50 or < 0, Score = -1	
2	P/ FCF1	< 12, Score = 1	>30 or < 0, Score = -1	
3	P/S1	< 0.8, Score = 1	< 0, Score = -1	

4	P/B[1]	< 1, Score = 1	< 0, Score = -1
5	Sales Q/Q	> 15%, Score = 1	< 0, Score = -1
	Compare quarter to quarter of last year		
6	EPS Q/Q	> 20% , Score = 1	< 0, Score = -1
			Grand Score
Stock Symbol	Current Price	SPY	
Date2			

Footnote.

1. Even with less chances, there is still a possibility of having negative values for Book, Equity, and Sales (because of accounting adjustments)
2. You should only put your information in the last row. SPY compares a stock's returns to that of others to tell you its chances of beating the market.

Score

All metrics are to be scored and once you're done with that, calculate the Grand Score by adding each score. It's considered a pass if we have 3 as the Grand Score and 2 represents that it's still worthy of further analysis. The scores given by other vendors could be added as well.

Other Sources

You shouldn't go for a stock that has failing scores provided that there are more sources available. However, you'd either have to be their customer or have a subscription. Elevated insider purchases and other such new positive developments should also be enough for ignoring them.

Vendor	Grade	Fail
Fidelity	Analysts' Opinions	< 4
IBD	Composite	< 50
Value Line	Proj. 3-5 yr. return. Also its composite rating	< 3%
Zacks	Rank	5
Vector Vest	VST	< 0.7

There are high chances that your nearest library has Value Line and IBD. It can also be beneficial to use the Relative Pricing of IBD. It could also be possible that there is free analysis available in Vector Vest if there aren't too many stocks.

Very Basic Advices for Beginners

P/E, Debt/Equity, and Market Cap (capitalization) are some of them. Beginners are recommended to work with P/E between 5 and 20, Market Cap > 800 million, and Debt/Equity < .25 (25 percent) when not dealing with airlines, utilities, and other such debt-intensive industries. The source of this information is Finviz.com.

You can go with a single sector for less than 30% of your portfolio and one stock for less than 20% of your portfolio.

Also, stocks with below-average Fidelity scores should not be bought.

If you want to take the conservative route, you should have <1 beta, where the market S&P 500 index is represented by Beta=1. With this, you can say that if beta=1.5, the market develops to 50% more of its capacity.

You can get to know more about your skill set and strategies of trading stocks by trying out virtual trading where you use fake resources for trading stocks. Those who don't have this option can either go for spreadsheets or visit simulator.investopedia.com.

Fundamental Metrics

ROE

If you want to see the performance of your management, you should have a look at a vital financial indicator in ROE (short for return of equity). With that being said, it is no longer a viable option for prediction because of its extremely high usage.

If you want to determine the key fiscal upturns and downturns faced by the stock price, you can have a look at the firm's ROE for 5 years at minimum.

You can also compare the management of one company to other companies by drawing a comparison between its ROE to the sector's average ROE. There is a low average ROE for utilities and other such sectors.

Basically, Market Cap is the product of share price and the number of outstanding shares

Market Cap (Capitalization)

Market Cap = Total no. of outstanding shares * share price

Beginners should go for US stocks that have at least 800 million as their market cap. Even though conventions are subjective and should take into account inflation, following are the conventions of the present time period:

Class	Market Cap (million)
Nano Cap	< $50M
Micro Cap	$50M to $250M
Small Cap	$250M to $1B (billion)
Mid Cap	$1B to $10B
Large Cap (Blue Chip)	$10B to $50B
Mega Cap	>50B

The stock's risk is inversely proportion to the cap. Only the companies' owners and speculators have access to Micro Cap and Nano Cap, while skilled investors have access to Mid Cap and Small Cap since these caps' stocks are normally skipped by institutional investors. Moreover, institutional investors trade Mega Cap, Large Cap, and some Mid Cap. There is continuous research being performed on them.

My Metrics

I normally go with Debt Load/Equity, ROE, Free Cash Flow, Short percentage of outstanding shares, Analysts' Opinions, PEG, and Expected P/E.

Furthermore, I also take into account various shortened parameters from more than one source. An instance of this can be that I have access to a composite rank for fundamentals and momentum all thanks to my subscription services.

You can reduce your considered stocks by screening them using the parameters. I end up skipping the majority since small Chinese enterprises burn them a number of times.

Mid, High and Low Values of Common Metrics

Metric	Mid Range	Low Range	High Range
P/E (last 12 months)	< 10	>40	< 4
Price / Cash Flow	< 12	>30	< 4
Price / Sales	< 2.5	>3	< .2
Price / Book	< 2.0	>4	< .2
PEG	< 1.5	>2	< .2

While high range stands for low numbers in this table, it actually represents good values. However, it can be false on some occasions. On the other hand, poor values are represented by low range. This can be seen in a number of online stocks comprised P/E > 40 (poor) in the year 2000 whereas those with 3 P/E (that are supposedly good) were ignored bargain stocks in the year 2000. I would actually go with Mid Range. From P/E, it should fall within the range of 4-10. However, you can take into consideration the present market status and your own tolerance for adjusting this range. For a top market trend, you can have its range as 5-12 or anything similar. If you don't do that, you'd be all out of stocks for evaluating.

I have considered decade-long data for going with these values. With their help, it is possible to predict how a stock will perform in a year and the ranges should be checked on half-yearly basis in the market of today.

When it comes to stock price appreciation, it is possible to have superior prediction with the help of metrics having mid-range and high-range values. The table in consideration shows that the chances of the stocks having low-range values to encounter a fiscal loss are higher than other stocks in about 365 days. Rather than ROE and other such low values, it is possible for high values to actually be beneficial.

Nevertheless, there may be changes in the values' range. In cases where the stocks are not kept for even longer than a month or the market is driving toward momentum, there can be better prediction with price growth, PEG, and other momentum parameters. Checking the metrics category (Value and Growth) favored by the present market is necessary. It is possible to determine the present favorite through some subscription services or websites. Furthermore, you should have a look at how all the metrics are performing every 3-6 months. Moreover, the table has to be considered for adjusting the new range values.

Momentum parameters take about a single month, while fundamental ones take close to 6-12 months for materializing the performance. Apart from PEG, each metric is fundamental in our table. There is never any use of P/B without financial stocks.

Example of Searching with High Range Values

There could be risks involved with stocks having the majority of their parameters in low-range, like P/E = 40 in our table. Considering this, the stocks having mid-range metrics (for example, P/E = 10) are to be selected. However, the stocks with low-range metrics should be avoided.

In this example, we are taking stocks that have high P/B and P/E values. There are high chances that you'll only have a few stocks within this range.

E > 0 and

P/E < 4 and

P/B < .2

Where E represents earning for every share and the company has to make profits.

The firm probably has a problem (such as a legal notice) if there are high range value. A P/E < 4 is something you should suspect. With that being said, it is possible for very small companies to be solid since the market doesn't pay enough attention to them. Also, you should also work more on your evaluation of the stock and its sector.

When it comes to the following year, there are more chances of stocks within low-range to encounter a financial loss. Even though exceptions are possible, the statistics confirm this case. AMZN2 has high P/B and P/E and thus, this stock does not have value. Nonetheless, you won't be wrong to forget about these poor metrics for a company is working on improving its infrastructure and market share in order to find future success.

It should also be noted that companies that have a reputation and/or the ones like IBM that have been thoroughly research do not fit this parameter. A number of metric formulae have become obsolete since they ignore patents, intellectual properties, and market appeals like brand names.

Following is one way of searching for mid-range values.

$E > 0$ and

$P/E < 10$ and

$P/E > 4$

For this example, only the firms whose P/Es and positive earnings are between 4 and 10 exclusively are to be included. It is recommended to get a number of companies having mid-range P/Es.

Average volume, market cap, and minimum price are some of the filters that can be added. You should go easy on your criteria by taking mid-range values in the table to start in case you don't get enough stocks. However, you should do the exact opposite if you get excess stocks. In cases where one gets stocks normally with a screen but not in that particular day, what this implies is that it is not possible to get enough bargain stocks since the market is over-valued.

If you want to reduce the amount of stocks for further evaluation, you should begin with this. Stocks dealing with abnormal cases are not covered by your parameters. An example of this can be that IBM is still included even though it has been having a high P/B value for quite some time now.

The stocks to be analyzed can be reduced through the searches that consider fundamental metrics. At times, it can be a good idea not to score the stocks that are dealing with abnormal circumstances.

There should be a comparison between the metrics of the company and its sector average.

Since you're basically comparing the same thing, there's no going wrong with this comparison.

It is also a good idea to have a comparison between a company's metrics and the sector average. There's no use of having a comparison between the P/S of a supermarket and that of other sectors since the P/S of an average supermarket can be quite low. There's this requirement of a handsome amount of debt for utilities and other such sectors for running a firm.

Nevertheless, in cases where a sector's metrics (such as P/E) abruptly falls below its historical average, this implies that there is better value in the sector and/or the sector is out-of-favor.

What you're getting below is the comparison between Apple and its sector + a retail sector on a certain date as an example. Metrics are subject to change.

Metric	Apple	Computer	Retail
P/E	11	19	24
(5 year average)	16	17	15
PEG	.6	N/A	1.4
Price /Cash Flow	9.4	8.1	9.2
Price /Book	3.3	3.0	3.6
EPS Growth	-6%	-42%	2.6%
(last 5 years)	62%	45%	11%
Operating Margin	20%	15%	8%

ROE	30%	14%	19%
Debt / Equity	2%	7%	88%
Inventory Turnover	76%	53%	4.55x

When it comes to our table, some metrics can only be applied to an industrial sector (like computers for Apple). For this example, there should be a comparison between AAPL and Computer (instead of Retail).

From "Debt / Equity" and Inventory Turnover, it can be seen that the retail sector requires more borrowed money in comparison to the computer sector as an example.

Top-Down Approach

Firstly, the risks of the market need to be compared. Afterward, you should head over to a website like Finviz.com for selecting the best sector. Once you're done with that, there needs to be a comparison between the fundamental metrics of that sector's key stocks.

Some Metrics Do Not Apply

In terms of financial institutions, P/B can normally be more beneficial than P/CF. With that being said, it was determined in the year 2007 that the quality of loan (not present here) is the most significant parameter. Talking about retails, P/S can have more significance, while other sectors depend mostly on the expected P/E.

Compare Metrics to its Five-Year Average

You can call a company totally undervalued provided that it has five-year average P/E = 20 and it is 10 currently. Debt/equity and other likewise metrics are to be considered.

Growth Metrics

Earnings, sales, and stock price have their growth rates in the growth metrics, which can benefit growth investors.

There is high significance of earning growth rate for value investors as well. The reason for this is that the majority of stocks elevated their earnings growth, which resulted in a lot of gains. In cases where there's no change in the price (PEG) regardless of earning growth, there are high chances of price appreciation and it to go back to the historical average P/E.

Momentum Metrics

Growth depends on momentum metrics. Key metrics include the rates of increase of the volume, the stock price, and so on. Earning announcement seasons (a year features four of them) also has earnings revision. With the help of a subscription service, you can also get a composite rank named as Timely or anything like that. My momentum portfolio has its average holding period < 30 days for momentum strategies, so only these parameters were considered.

Insiders' Buying

There can be a lot of factors that influence the selling of stocks by insiders. You should pay attention to the instances where purchase multiple stocks from their companies with market price. Insiders have the most knowledge about how their firms and their industries are doing.

Visit Finviz.com or other such site and choose insiders' purchases. Afterward, skip the option exercises. According to my preference, the purchases from multiple insiders and high ratios of Net Total Purchase Value/Market Cap are better. However, you should make sure that the insider didn't sell a similar valued stock before purchasing the stocks.

You can get this information from OpenInsider.

InsiderSights is another top one and it has advanced options that could have a learning curve.

Where to Get Metrics?

Free or affordable websites like Finviz.com, Fidelity.com (requires registration), AAII (quite affordable), and your broker's site can provide this info.

Stock Screen 123, Vector Vest, Zacks, IBD, and Value Line are some of the more expensive options, but their subscriptions don't cost more than a grand per year. There is duplication of a lot of data provided by multiple vendors. So, it is better to focus on only 1-2 sources.

You can also get access to composite metrics like timing (for price appreciation rate, PEG, Technical Analysis indications, etc.) and value (for debt, P/E, etc.) through various vendors.

Finviz.com provides a helpful metric in short %. Fidelity customers can select Research and afterward Stock. Press Detailed after entering the stock name. According to my opinion, there are great advantages of the Analysts' Opinions by Fidelity.

Through Finviz.com, you can get free access to sufficient useful info. Moreover, there's a screen feature as well. By clicking Help, you can have a look at the website's features and the parameters considered.

CHAPTER 10

WHY BEAR MARKET IS DIVIDEND INVESTOR'S BEST FRIEND?

If there's a market condition where there's a 20%+ drop in the security prices from their peak, it's called a bear market. Also, there will be a further drop. Normally, we see that bear markets have 33% decline. In comparison to the normal correction (where there's a 10% pullback), bear market conditions are far worse. There's this expectation of a correction after one or two years. With that being said, I never said that you'll be affected by this market condition. Actually, investors typically see a bear market a lot in their careers. However, when this condition occurs remains unknown. Apart from that, you'll find that the majority of portfolios will start getting relatively under-valued, which is caused as the number of sellers becomes greater than that of buyers. However, it might be upsetting for investors who rely on constant market growth. On the other hands, those following smart money know that they'll get top-notch buying opportunities because of a bear market. What can be tough for investors is to find the right time of getting out prior to the bear and getting back in when the market hits its bottom. Investors working on the smart money should estimate how long an average market cycle lasts and then consider market indicators for timing it.

There's no telling when a bear market will end. However, this condition typically exists for 14 months prior to a new bull. On the other hand, the majority of 10% correction doesn't take too long to be taken care of as they normally last for 1-2 months. With that being said, the life-span of a correction can significantly increase if it doesn't actually turn into a bear market. In 1959-1960, there was a 14% decline in the market, which experienced a new bull after 422 days of correction. The market was even closer to experiencing a bear in 1976-1978 when there was a 19% decline in the market and the recovery required 531 days.

It is possible for corrections to be puzzling since the investor wouldn't know if it's merely a correction or a bear market's starting point. There are high chances that an investor will turn into a speculator in case there's no quick resolution to the correction. One might get confused whether to pull money or buy the dip. However, you need not worry with this idea. You know you can only consider profits of long-term market cycles and ignore market conditions for making your decisions. So, you will initially have to get to know more about the working of a bear market and eliminate its fear from your heart. There's no downside to a bear market; instead, you should be expecting such events to take place in the life of an investor. Once you've understood this concept, you will see that dividend investors actually benefit from such conditions, even more when they occur in the early stages.

 The previous parts cover the mean's reversion and how buying a stock less than its 200-days moving average can benefit you. A bear market affects both individual stocks and the majority of indexes with less than their 200-days moving average for quite some time. We aren't focusing on making a return at the bottom by timing our exit from a top because this move could be negatively influenced by human emotions and errors. With that being said, you can more easily ensure the cheapness of securities at the time of a full bear market and you can also be in a position to decide if you want to hold that security for more than 5 years, however, one must be careful when making decisions during this kind of trend.

Strong yields can be quite favorable for dividend investors. Another thing that such investors follow is patience since strong investments with increasing yield on an annual basis are preferred over speculative ones with high yields on the same day. The lower the dividend yield, the higher the stock price. Considering this, there's an increment in a new investment's yield at the time of a bear. For this, however, it is assumed that the firms haven't reduced their dividends because of such fiscal circumstances. Even though it can be true for a few companies, there are high chances that new investors will get better dividend yields because of the prices decline in case you're buying the Dividend Aristocrats, the S&P 500, or any other index having great hold of the market. Individuals reducing their dividend will be balanced out by the stocks of the S&P 500. Moreover, the Dividend Aristocrats companies are more likely to increase their dividend via both advantageous and disadvantageous economic circumstances.

If you buy securities at the time of a bear, you won't have to wait much for your initial investment to start getting a stronger yield. When the stock has hit rock bottom, it is possible to enter with a cheap price and high yield. Because of this move, you'll be getting both better capital gains and dividend payments.

There's no better opportunity than a bear market for people interested in building a portfolio. You wouldn't have to pay much attention to your earlier investments and just look at your new ones prospering in the market. On the other hand, you'll be getting dividend income in case of existing investments. Although seeing your portfolio's value depreciating wouldn't be a pleasure, it makes for the perfect opportunity to reinvest those dividends. If you recall what we learned earlier, it can be really beneficial to compound our dividends throughout our trading year.

It is possible to get 40 shares in case you invest you a grand out of your dividend income in a security with selling price of $25/share. However, all thanks to a bear market that reduces the price to $20, it will be possible for 50 shares to be bought for the same grand.

1,000 / 25 = 40

1,000 / 20 = 50

You need to pay attention that dividends work on pay-per-share. This means that if the quarterly dividend of the security equals $0.3, then you'll be getting $12 in quarterly payments with a 4.8% yield since the security's selling price equals $25.

(0.30 x 4) / 25 = 4.8%

40 x 0.30 = 12

If the security gets to $20, you'll be getting $15 in quarterly payments since there's a 6% yield from your new investment.

 (0.30 x 4) / 20 = 6.0%

50 x 0.30 = 15

Additionally, if there's a bear and you reinvest your dividends, you can make $3 more which don't just stop there. Since the market faced a decline, each quarter will give you $3 more. There's a way to make another $3/per quarter by ensuring that the market hasn't recovered and reinvesting a grand in dividend income (by a grand, I mean $1015. Another benefit is that you'll start getting distributions as dividend reinvestments also consider your additional $3.

Let's switch the circumstances: assume that the market went up and the security increased to 30$ in place of $25 per share. In this case, you'd only be getting 33 shares for your $1000 dividend income with $9.90 as the quarterly distribution. It's no mystery why someone would go for compounding $15/quarter throughout their lifespan instead of $9.90/quarter. However, we would still accept the $9.90 if given. There are chances that the market can go up, so you should not wait for a better entry point. What you should do is ignore the market conditions and focus on reinvesting the dividends at the determined time frames. In case of a bear market, you need not worry since you're making the most out of your reinvested dividends.

These $3 may not seem much, but you'll be getting an extra $5.1/quarter (15.00 – 9.90 = 5.10) since there's been a decline in the market. You'll be making $612 as your dividend income (5.10 x 4 x 30 = 612) in case you retire after 30 years. Although this doesn't seem like a lot of money, note that you'll also get compound additional returns of this extra $612 in the future. If you want to increase your wealth, you'll have to take such small steps. The only thing keeping you away from gathering a lot of wealth is not making such money moves repetitively. You'll make an extra $3,672 instead of just $612 in case the duration of the bear equals 1.5 years (612 x 6 = 3,672).

In addition, you'll also save some fees money by going for the best index funds and commission money by going for an online discount broker rather than a full-service financial advisor. Your holdings will also get increased dividends after 365 days. You'll do well by taking such small initiatives again and again for quite some time. Your returns are mainly driven by your investments in strong asset classes. However, you can benefit even more by taking such small steps repeatedly. Apart from the small steps, we will also be taking a look at the bigger steps that you can take in Chapter 11-12, which deals with asset allocation and rebalancing. With that being said, a bear market comes with extra ammunition and it's the perfect time you understand it.

You can easily notice how exactly you can exploit a bear marker. Firstly, you can buy securities at a lesser price. Secondly, new purchases have dividend yields with more strength. Also, throughout your lifespan (or any chosen time frame), you'll be gathering larger distributions produced by your new securities. Indeed, there are a lot of advantages of a bear market, but such declines can also come with drastic measures. With that being said, you shouldn't only look at the negative side of things like the majority of investors do.

The deeper you get into your investment horizon, the stronger the damages you'll encounter from a bear market in case you don't rely on increasing allocation to bonds. Maintaining exposure to equities is also necessary when it comes to acquiring frequent benefits from market increase. Risk and reward also have its significance in this case. Although you'll more easily be able to handle a market upturn by allocating a lot to equities, it is smart to still be ready. In case of a bear, the equities will be reduced to a tremendous extent. Under these circumstances, you don't have to do a thing. What's most important is that you don't unload under its pressure. You won't encounter any worse selling conditions than those at the time of a bear market.

If you face a bear market in the beginning of your career and haven't accumulated much wealth, you have a chance of increasing your holdings without spending too much prior to getting to the point where you have such a big portfolio that it can be affected by the bear. However, if you've gathered a lot of holdings, this will change a lot of things. Also, it would be more difficult for you to see the bear in its entirety. With that being said, it is possible to take advantage of a bear at this point as well. On the other hand, there won't be a lot of time to gather those bigger dividend yields resulting from new investments under a bear.

We're not done with bear markets yet as we'll return to this topic later on in our investment strategy, but we'll be considering asset allocation, dollar-cost averaging, and rebalancing the portfolio this time. Furthermore, we'll also see the significance of bear markets in the lifespan of our different holdings.

CHAPTER 11

HOW TO BUILD DIVIDEND PORTFOLIO?

Regardless of the type of market, investors will get the most help from their previous experiences for saving for retirement with the passage of their career and life. It's pretty simple: you can't play the game if you don't know the rules. If anyone does so, they will not only be beaten in an instant but other players will exploit them as well.

For investors to build a dividend stocks-related portfolio, they'll have to have knowledge about building an income and the ways it will take care of their expenses after they've hung up their boots for quite some time. It takes some time to reap the benefits from dividend investing, but it's still better than a risky plan that guarantees fast cash. Accordingly, you'd have to put in tens of years in this type of investing and also know about the starting point and the ways of establishing a dividend portfolio.

Knowing Risks of Inflation

Investors must be aware of the probable effects of inflation risk on their investment made in different companies. Inflation is defined as the constant increment in the cost of goods and services for a long term. The effects of inflation on each company may vary and hence inflation affects every investor differently depending on the company in which he invested.

The investment decision is to be made very cautiously, analyzing all the expected risk and its possible effects on any venture. Specialists consider market risk and rate of inflation before making any investment decision; the risk involved also depends on how diversified their portfolio is. This is a very crucial step as it determines long term earnings for the investor.

For instance, if an investor maintains a portfolio of $1 million with a dividend rate of 5%, then the investor will expect an income of $50,000 per year, which can save the investor from adverse market conditions. However, if the inflation rate increases to 3% allowing the investor to have the purchasing power of $35,000 in 12 year time and on adding the tax of 30% the investor will be left with the amount of $25,000 to spend at the completion of 12 years.

Benefits of Market Growth

To understand the reason to invest in the dividends, it is necessary to understand the related risks. Dividend portfolio is always subject to non-guaranteed dividends and other adverse economic events as explained in the paragraphs above where there was a list of equities which paid a dividend at 4% yield.

Generally, the dividend payout ratio has an increase of 3% per year that compensates for the inflation and increases most likely at the annual rate of 5% during those 12 years. If the mentioned situation actually occurs then the initial earning of $50,000 will increase to $90,000 per year, however, this would come to $62,000 if the inflation rate reaches 3%. And the tax of 15% (Subject to change) can make the income worth $53,000.

When the investor is able to implement both the techniques, it results in a protection against the adverse effect of inflation and any changes in the stock exchange market. Diversity in portfolio such as including both bonds and stocks will help the investor earn a reasonable income without much danger of dividend risks.

Remember to Keep Safety in Mind

As you are always taught to step cautiously while crossing the road, to avoid any mishap, similarly it is highly advised to analyze all the expected risks before planning to invest and expand the dividend portfolio. The first step is to design a methodology, which will include a detailed analysis of the companies you have selected to invest in and then to patiently wait for the right time to make the investment in the shares of the respective company.

Patience is required in making the selection of the Investee Company and then choosing the correct price to invest in. This will increase the chances to enhance profitability. For instance, to wait for blue-chip stocks which provides dividend at the rate of 4-5% or even more as traced from their respective balance sheet.

You can never completely avoid the risks, you can only mitigate the risks- some risks are in control, while others are uncontrollable, it is recommended to the investor to make an adequate selection before investment to mitigate risks. One example of the risk is a yield trap. Companies offering a high yield rate with a poor balance sheet position show that these companies cannot provide with consistent yield, but the high yield rate attract the investors even if they will not be able to give them a consistent income. It appeals apparently but will result in reduced dividend incomes in the longer run.

Steps to Building Dividend Portfolio

1. **Create Diversity in Your Portfolio with at least 25 Solid Stock Options**

Investment does not mean becoming a billionaire overnight. Investors can only be successful if they develop their portfolio slowly over time to reap its benefits in the long run such as at the time of retirement. This implies slow and steady wins the race. You require time and consistency and need to focus on getting dividends with no fear of losing your investments.

2.   Diversity among Multiple Industries

Investors should wisely diverse their portfolio to not risk all their fortune in a single venture. For instance, if you have invested all your capital in different companies from a single industry, for example, the oil industry, if the oil prices fell down to $10 per barrel this would have a huge impact on your earnings and your dividend income will get a negative hit. The solution to this problem is to diversify the portfolio.

3.   Financial Stability is More Important than Growth

The investor needs to prioritize; first preference shall be relying on the company's health to provide dividend income consistently and with a gradual increase over the period of time, instead of depending on the abrupt growth of the stocks. To do this, it is recommended to have a close check on the credit ratings of the Companies. The Value Line survey generally has a scale to grade the stocks from A++ to Ds; stocks with ratings of A are opted for by successful investors as they carry the lowest proportion of risk.

4.   Focus on Companies That Have History of Raising Their Dividends

Here are some tips to be followed before investing in the enhancement of a dividend portfolio. Bank of America offered dividend at the rate of 4% in early 1995 that amounted to 47 cents per share. However, the purchase back of the shares at the time was $11.2 per share which increased the dividend to $2.12 in 2006 allowing the investor to earn 18.9% above stock's actual cost. For finding such companies, you can scan the list of S&P's "Dividend Aristocrats – which have been providing increasing dividend for continuously 25 years – and Mergent's "Dividend Achievers" – which are in the 10th year of continuous rise in dividends.

5.   Look for Companies That Have Modest Payout Ratios

Successful investors calculate relevant ratios to assess the position of the Company, payout ratios are determined from the dividend as a proportion of accumulated earnings. If the ratio is calculated as 60% or low that means the Company cannot sustain itself in case of any economic crisis. It is, therefore, most suitable to invest in a company that has a strategy to face the unforeseeable events and safeguard the stakeholders against it.

6.   Reinvest What You Earn from Your Dividends

If an investor keeps on reinvesting the money earned as dividend income to extract a fairly large amount at the retirement age, the dividends can multiply at an unexpected rate without any additional effort.

Biggest Mistakes to Avoid When Growing Your Portfolio

As the yields and bonds are very low nowadays, they have lost the attraction and investors are now more inclined towards investment in dividend income. Moreover, investors seeking a sustainable source of income at their retirement also invest in dividend-paying stocks for a more reliable earning which increases over the time.

Earnings from dividends are majorly attracting the people approaching their retiring age and one of the major reasons for the increased inclination of investors toward dividend income is because fixed income has reached the lowest levels.

It cannot be said, that investing in dividend payout stocks is the safest option as the stock market is always subject to unpredictable economic conditions. San Francisco advising company, Forward Management issued a report titled "How Not to Invest in Dividend Stocks" which explained various pitfalls in a dividend portfolio.

Chasing Those Big Yield Goals

If the stock is offering a very lucrative dividend rate it is highly possible that these rates will not be maintained by the company in the longer term and will hence not always be the best option to get high returns. High dividend payouts cannot remain consistent for more than a year; thereby huge fluctuations can be witnessed in the company's financial position because when the company faces an economic crisis, it needs to curtail the dividend pay-out ratio to meet the financial needs for progress in future.

"The companies with sustainable and successful positions were the ones knowing the technique to offer the combination of appealing dividend ratios with comparatively low payout ratios; this was based on the study of accumulated data of several years from various global markets". Ruff wrote.

Ruff also stated that "A company offering a payout ratio within a range of 30%-60% will be successful in making a consistent dividend distribution among its shareholders. Simultaneously, the ratio shall be not high enough to provide an opportunity to reinvest the funds for incremental internal growth, also termed as consumption of the power of compounding interest".

Relying on Overly Mechanical Investment Plans

These methodologies ignore the basic fluctuations and dividend policy changes, which may impact the investor's dividend income flow. The same has occurred multiple times in Europe where several telecommunication companies which made payments to the shareholders through dividend had higher yields exceeding more than 100%, which is a condition to be alert, as the rates are excessively high and are more likely to crash in near future.

Ignoring Variety of Growth Factors

To be successful, investors need to analyze company's health to estimate its progress and rise in addition to the dividend yields that it offers- this is because the company's potential to grow can give comfort to the investor to have a consistent dividend income over the long run, which allows him to enjoy the fruits from the invested amount at the retirement age.

For instance, we will assume an investor with a portfolio of $1 million and yearly expenses of $50,000. If the portfolio's yield rate is 3% annual, then the investor will be in possession of less than 50% of the initial balance after 2 decades. After another decade, the investor will have a diminishing balance. But, if the same portfolio yield profit at the rate of 7% then the investor would have saved about $3 million after the same time of three decades.

Showing Favoritism to Home Market

There are many opportunities available to the investors to invest capital abroad, in countries having a progressing economy as they will be offering dividends at higher rates than those being offered by the companies in the U.S.

It is very important to spread the portfolio by including stock of companies established in the progressing economies, thereby enhancing the portfolio by investing in international markets. For instance, businessmen has initiated to take cloud operations abroad, specifically to African nations based on the increasing demand in those countries .The examples are Amazon and VMware.

In two decades time, those markets have captured 47% of the global gross domestic product by increasing their shares of the global economy.

Focused Towards Those Blue Chips

It is usually believed by the investors that it is more secure to invest in blue-chip companies' dividend stocks, however, it will be more costly to purchase those stocks and they won't be offering significant yields like smaller stocks. Stocks of blue-chip companies give an opportunity to avail liquidity benefits but limited chances to expect an increment in yield. Blue-chips stocks being overly-priced have moved out of the scope of investors as investing in such stocks will leave no room for diversification of stocks

Following What Everyone Else is Doing

There are plenty of dividend funds that are driven by the records that can make what is called benchmark-hugging, where portfolios are overexposed to those bigger name organizations and stocks while not giving us a lot of consideration regarding the littler organizations that may have a superior arrangement of chances.

Giving Macro Factors More Weight

Investment is always subject to risks that can never be completely avoided because of the emergent markets that offer fascinating potential particularly in countries that are likely to experience an upsurge like European, Middle Eastern and African countries. These regions may give numerous opportunities to earn huge profits and effectively execute local operations which are not possibly influenced by worldwide trends.

For instance, because of the current economic crisis, the stock market in Europe is not as profitable as before, creating suspicion among investors. Yet, there must be few companies, whose stocks are still performing well in the market and can offer dividends, which will help in keeping the portfolio in a better position.

CHAPTER 12

MANAGING YOUR PORTFOLIO

Diversification

One of the best recommendations for mitigation of risks related to the investment portfolio is to diversify the investment in different industries. This implies investing the only particular amount in a specific venture say 5% of the total available capital, along with 15% limit of investment in that particular industry. It is also recommended to avoid investing in a company so much so that from that particular single company you earn more than 15% of the total dividend income from your portfolio; this is because if you earn 20-25% of total dividend income from a particular company, you will have a huge impact on your portfolio if the company ever faces any problems and stops offering a dividend, or cuts down the rate of dividend. Similarly, an investor should consider the risk of investing in companies of the same industry in an ETF or closed-end fund. Investors shall always be cautious in making an investment if any crisis to a particular company or an industry could adversely affect the dividend income (like 20-30% devaluation of the portfolio). The investor is not only responsible to safeguard the revenue stream but also to maintain the value of the portfolio.

Expansion of portfolio must be done with consideration to balance between stocks in local and international markets. An investor who relies on dividend income must protect himself from the risks associated with emergent market stocks. European stocks in themselves are not susceptible to high risk but the exchange risk of the currencies can increase the associated risks. The ultimate solution to the matter is to invest a fair amount in U.S. stocks of multinational companies who earn huge revenues from the performance of the setups in abroad. It is not wise to invest in stocks just for the purpose of diversification. The basic purpose of an investor is to earn huge revenue and be at low risk. If your core aim is to defeat the market (then all the best wishes for that) but practically you cannot do that if you over-expand your portfolio because then your portfolio will itself be representing the stock market.

Volatility of Stock or Portfolio

Expansion and staying away from volatility diminishes risk. Volatility is affected by various events happening in business, for example, changes in accumulated income, financing costs, work efficiency and in the long run net profit. This essential volatility of net profits is amplified by market variations in P/E proportions. The volatility of the P/E ratio has a positive co-relation with expected future profits. P/E ratio of 20 is the maximum range acceptable by the dividend investor; however, the rapidly progressing business sectors may sell at P/E ratio exceeding 20. For an increasingly steady, trudging, entrenched customer staple stock, during times of generally speaking cynicism, the P/E proportion may tumble to 8-10 and even lower for less secure, previous high flying development stocks. Total market normal P/E in the long term is around 15-16.

To reduce volatility, you need to hold on the stocks with lower beta numbers, having safety factors of 1 or 2 and having high rankings on their financial strength as these are the essentials for the stocks that are comparatively steady. One of the options to mitigate the volatility is to make the right decision while purchasing the stock. One of the main features to be considered to make the right purchase decision is to observe if the stock is at its lowest price when compared with its price data historically. Insecurity and lust can influence the cost of share and investor needs to show bravery in making purchase decision when fear thrives. It is necessary to assess the nature of the fear, whether it is of the long term due to prolonged adverse impact or short term which will disappear within a year or two.

The discussion and proofs given above shake the pillars of the theory that explains that the market is continuously efficient and that prices reflected by the market always show the true worth of stock. Equity costs are subject to discount every now and then which is the time an investor is patiently waiting to execute the transaction. If the stock market was as efficient as discussed theoretically by many educationalists then it would have never required any experience and anyone could purchase the stock at any time without considering any risks. Market inefficiency can be understood completely through a history of the high/low turning points in the history of the S&P 500 index price since 1929.

Market volatility is to be understood so that the investor can determine the point of time when the purchase is to be made (that is when the expected prices are low) and the point of time when stocks are to be sold (that is when the expected prices are high). Volatility is higher when there is variation in the Federal Reserve Bank discount rate or at each quarterly end when the variation is made in portfolio by the mutual funds to provide the names of investments that performed better in each 3-monthly report.

Timing

Majority of warnings regarding the market timing risks are genuine. Hence, it is better to be careful and have some information about market timing to avoid such risks.

With respect to changes in the Federal Reserve rebate rate, nearly every rise in the rate prompts the finish of a positively trending market. Try not to battle the market pattern whether it is up or down.

On the off chance that you locate a stock worth purchasing during a general falling market or falling profit, it might be clever to invest half of your investment. You may effectively have the option to buy the second half for less sometime in the not too distant future. On the off chance that there is some terrible news about a firm whose stock you claim or wish to purchase, there are chances of further decline of the stock The insiders at firm will try in such a situation to conceal the true story from public as long as possible so as to dump their own possessions before the full release of the news that can further aggravate the stock pricing.

Usually, the complete annual gain is observed between Novembers and Mays by the overall stock market. This is because of the higher cash inflow received by the public at large and all investing organizations in the form of upcoming investment capital, deferred tax amount for retirement accounts, bonuses and additional occasions near year-end. It is better if the investor fully invests in the capital before the peak period is reached. This recalls me of the popular saying among investors, "sell in May, and then leave the market."

From 1929-2009, the Dow Jones 30 stocks saw eleven significant twists in market direction. The time length between these twists ranged from two years to 26 years. In any case, most of these twists were separated by six years. In the event that you are cautious in the price paid for a decent consistent profit paying stock, you will soon get a chance to reach the no-profit-no-loss position.

There are no additional efforts needed to hold the securities endlessly, however, this will expose you to all the market risks as you will be part of the market all the time. But you can survive with that. There are plenty of examples in the U.S.; forefathers of many of the rich families did the same. However, losses in dividend income and the diminishing value of the portfolio were easily covered-up by the high income of these families. You can opt to hold stocks for the long term if the dividend income earned from them is enough for you to meet the needs and expenses and you don't have enough time or curiosity to assess the investments.

The decision of stock sale and reinvestment of the dividend earned is highly influenced if a person's only source of income is the dividend income, by the distribution guidelines from your private IRA or 401K retirement accounts if you have crossed the age of 70. The utilization of these retirement accounts shall be kept near the IRS minimum. If you desire to keep your stocks forever then you shall not utilize more than 4-5% of annual invested capital to meet your expenses, this will keep your portfolio in line with the inflation. Endeavor a touch of timing right now, with your retirement accounts. Frequently, however not generally, selling prices of the shares might tempt you in late spring or December and you will end up selling the securities within the time period to earn the best price against the securities. A superior intend to abstain from selling shares at low costs while fulfilling the base required yearly withdrawal from your IRA is partition the absolute yearly sum into four a balance of that is pulled back in mid-January, mid-April, mid-August, and mid-December. You can along these lines stay away from the riskiest period of September and October.

Whenever you decide to purchase any security, you shall answer to yourself, "can I comfortably hold the securities for 10-15 years?", so that you can cope up with any long-termed, rough market periods, this is crucial in case of a fund. It is not necessary to hold the securities for that long in reality, but it is only the comfort level you are ought to have with the securities.

Buy Considerations

When we talk about investing, there is no science behind it, but only arts. The features that can add to the beauty of this art are age and related experience. To achieve the point of proficiency, the risk is to be undertaken, but fear overcomes most of the investors and they lose patience after a loss and divert to purchase of bonds and CDs only to safeguard their earnings. In this way, they lose the opportunity to maintain a portfolio that could result in dividend earnings worth double to the cost of the portfolio they could have maintained 3-4 decades back. Studies as mentioned in this book and other related books can only give you some guidelines and techniques to be followed, but to master the actual art; you need to practical experience the business.

One "framework" of purchasing is designated "dollar-cost averaging." You invest the equivalent fixed dollar to a stock or a reserve each quarter or year or month. Much of the time, your normal expense per share is lower than the normal cost. However, I had a bad experience of this framework Despite the fact that you are purchasing fewer securities when costs are high perhaps you ought not to purchase any securities at that cost. At the point when you see a profitable venture and the cost is correct, submit at any rate half, if not 100% of your capital to it. Would you prefer this gradual cost variance method to purchase another income paying venture, say a high rise building? A similar chance of overpaying can happen in programmed dividend reinvestment programs. You may spare a modest sum on this commission-free buying, yet you will more likely be overpaying eventually in time. Purchasing any venture at a deal or close to deal cost is probably the most noteworthy need for successful investment.

A deep analysis of the dividend data and forecast of the projected future dividend increase can aid you in choosing a successful stock and emergent dividend. Rate of dividend and pay-out ratio shall be assessed to understand if the ratios will remain consistent economic crisis? To make a wise choice, it is essential for you to be informed of all the related news, and offerings by value line. To be prudent you shall adjust the risk factor in the projected future performance of the securities. Another need to be taken care of is the safeguard of the available capital. If you experience a major downfall in the cost of one of the securities, it is most likely there is some problem faced by the firm, but you need to analyze the term for which the problem may persist. If the problem will remain for the short term you are suggested to purchase at a discounted price.

While considering buying any security you are recommended to utilize a large-sized firm with good performance through the internet because in this way you will save your cost of $20-25 on every transaction until you reach a particular number of securities. I personally use Vanguard online brokerage service; they offer the best competitive cost of $7 for all sizes transaction and fast and effective completion of orders. Generally, my trades are "at the market", however, I use "limit order" when the securities are lightly traded, specifically when the spread of over 1% is shown between "bid" and "ask". I will not recommend utilizing the option of stop-loss orders as an unexpected and small decline in cost can result in a huge loss with respect to your holdings.

Asset Allocation

The primary subject of importance here is the sum or level of your assets that you will keep as current assets i.e. liquid in your money market brokerage sweep account. This is the place where profits and money acquired from sales are cleared as they are acquired. Numerous guides advocate keeping 5%-10% of your complete speculation capital in your liquid money market fund as this will save you from being bankrupted when it comes to meeting the daily routine expenses and making abrupt investments to seize the opportunity in case of "scream bargaining". I also maintain my liquid assets at the rate of 2% when great purchase opportunities are available in the securities exchange and the prevailing money market interest rates are very low as they are now (2010) almost negligible. During the period when money market interest rates were high (the 1980s) of over 10%, it would have been insightful to keep more assets in your money market sweep account, yet you should still be having sufficient amount for investment so as to avail the profit of money market that escalated quickly. In the uncommon occasions of emptying, keeping more money available is a decent decision. In the monetary examination, the sum or rates you should keep in your currency advertise is an individual issue. In the event that you might be confronted with supplanting your vehicle or the rooftop on your home sooner rather than later, that will greatly affect your decision. I'm an adherent to being completely contributed at practically all occasions as opposed to attempting to time the market with major money save for buys. Time after time the market flees from you while you are sitting tight at a decent cost.

Even portfolio maintained by equity investors is adjusted in accordance with the circumstances but in any case, the proportion of equities in a portfolio is not reduced below half. Your portfolio should consist of a small proportion of bonds and other fixed-income securities. Few market specialists have categorized various securities as bonds .These include investments like securities issued by electric utility organizations, REITs and energy limited firms. But, I do not agree with this categorization. In the time of economic crisis securities issued by these organizations and firms might result in an unexpected dividend reduction; due to the presence of this contingency, consistent earnings cannot be expected from the securities and thereby cannot be taken as a bond substitute which always provides with confirmed interest income.

CHAPTER 13

HOW TO REBALANCE YOUR DIVIDEND PORTFOLIO

Investors with a dividend portfolio shall continuously observe the circumstances and adjust the portfolio accordingly. This constant observation allows an investor to buy and sell his shares when the market is favorable, thereby, resulting in stable progress. This is usually the case of index investments and can also provide profitability equal to that of dividend payments.

To help investors in controlling the emotions prevalent in unstable market conditions the most helpful solution is to adjust the dividend portfolio. To make a profitable investment, an investor's decision shall be wise and diverse to be fruitful in long term, which means being an investor you shall be hard-working, persistent, and aiming to be focused on your plan instead of opting for short cuts to earn easy money.

Establish Your Targets

Initially, you shall plan your objectives, what you need from your investments and what securities should be included in the portfolio to help you earn it. Planning objectives will help you determine the industries and businesses in which you need to invest, particularly if you are an investor who aims to have a diverse portfolio of more than 30 differentiating securities. It is near to impossible to target each security, so a practical approach is to determine the industry and then project your discrete decisions on their performance.

The number of companies to be chosen as an investee from various selected industries depends on the investor- an investor can either choose to invest in more than 10 companies or to invest in one or two companies. The number of companies to be selected is purely dependent on the comfort level of the investor with the industry. Yet, it is also important that you not invest all your capital in one specific industrial sector as this will be very risky and can adversely affect the expected profitability from your portfolio.

For instance, you select following industries to invest in: financial (15%); utilities (15%); telecommunications (15%); energy (10%); healthcare (10%); housing (10%); retail goods (10%); technology (5%); public transport (5%); and bonds (5%).

On making such investments the investor will have reliability on the progression rate of the investee companies e.g. financial institutions like banks, utilities, and high tech companies due to increasing demand in mobile technology. The other selected sectors are based on the interest of the investor but since the investor would like to keep the risk level low they will invest more in the sectors from which he can have bigger and steady profits.

Select Rebalancing Trigger

While a few investors utilize a once-a-year trigger, numerous investors observe their stock movements several times in a year rather than observing on annual basis; several specialists also recommend observing the stocks at least on a quarterly basis. This is because of various transactional fees related to the investing business that might at times be favorable or unfavorable, but to benefit from the movement in the fees can be availed only if the stocks are observed on regular basis.

It is recommended to observe particular securities for at least 3 months before deciding on the investment this is because of the frequent movement in the stocks; the securities can be a profit in a month and in a loss in the other month. There is a famous guideline, "Sell in May and go away" which can be taken as advice to sell securities in the month of May to ignore upcoming expected adverse events until the month of November arrives when the stock market becomes stable and profitable again.

The other factor that needs to be observed to determine the adjustment of your dividend portfolio is an assessment of the rate of difference for every industry. If your objective is to have a 10 percent investment in transportation, you can accept the variation of 3% (increase and decrease) and within this estimated range you can make respective transactions. The test originates when you have to adjust investments made in all the different sectors and not just a single sector– a few specialists prescribe utilizing the option to sell for the cash or contribute extra funds.

Decide How You Will Rebalance Your Portfolio

Adjustment of the dividend portfolio doesn't necessarily mean that you have to give up securities against money. Often, it simply involves adding more funds to arrange and rebalance the rates among different sectors in a portfolio.

It is absurd if the investor sells 10 securities for $100 and then pays commission expense of $10. Adjustment of the dividend requires detailed and cautious planning which might fail due to quick and abrupt decisions.

Assume that the portfolio has a value of more than $100,000 and the majority of the investments are of $5,000 at the minimum. Now, if the transaction gives $1,000 only then the mentioned commission fee will be considered negligible and affordable, this means a deviation of 10-20% is acceptable in the portfolio.

Do So within Each Sector

Watch out for every one of the divisions spoke to in your profit portfolio and break down in the case of anything that should be changed inside and not as much on a wide scale. On the off chance that you claim stocks in six banks under the money related area, there may be a chance to rebalance between both of them depending on when you purchased the stocks.

In the end, the stocks that are doing admirably should be sold for a benefit that would then be able to be reinvested in the other existing banks in your portfolio. Or then again you could include two or three different organizations that have given some extraordinary potential for making your portfolio significantly more grounded. Ordinarily, when a financial specialist settles on this kind of option, they are placing their cash in a bank that is giving more grounded, progressively reliable yields rather than one in their portfolio that wasn't doing its fair share.

A few specialists would suggest holding up until the stock has arrived at a specific point over the first buying cost – like around the 20 to 25 percent point. At that point, a speculator is prescribed to assess the time expected to assemble that benefit and contrast it with different stocks in the portfolio.

CHAPTER 14

USING OPTIONS FOR INCOME

Profits aren't the best way to procure cash off the portions of stock you hold. You can likewise acquire cash by writing options contracts in case you don't avoid high risks. In truth, the risk is generally low and you can get a strong salary from selling options contracts. Likewise, you could join options with different methods for contributing to expanding your salary potential. For instance, you could put resources into a stock that delivered a strong profit and reinvests the profits over the long haul. In any case, you could even now make money from the offers by composing secured call options on them. Nonetheless, you must know that if there is a risk, you would need to sell the offers. The genuine risk is moderately low for two reasons. The first is that a couple of call options are really worked out, and the second is that despite being compelled to sell your offers, you will even now most likely make a benefit and can reinvest the returns from the deal in another stock.

What is Call Option?

A call option is an option to purchase portions of stock at a fixed cost. We consider the fixed value of the strike cost. An option accompanies a termination date, and there is a wide scope of lapse dates, however commonly, they will terminate in the close to a term like 3 weeks or a month. Hidden any options contract are portions of stock, and there are 100 portions of stock for every option agreement.

Options contracts can be exchanged on trades that are set up explicitly only for them, so there is a whole universe of options merchants living off the financial exchange. This attempts to further your potential benefit. The explanation is that most option merchants are keen on benefitting off the exchanging of the options contracts themselves; however, they aren't generally that keen on owning the portions of stock. Be that as it may, know that a few people who purchase options contracts are keen on purchasing the offers, so you may wind up selling your offers in certain conditions. Notwithstanding, the information shows this doesn't occur more often than not, thus as we'll see, this gives a chance to gain a month to month salary from your offers.

Pricing of Options

To begin with, you ought to acquaint yourself with certain options in the commercial center so you know how they are valued and you can get a thought of how a lot of cash you can make off your offers. To compose an option contract, you should claim in any event 100 portions of the fundamental stock. The cost of the option will fluctuate on two things; it will change on the cost of the fundamental stock itself, however, recall that the option likewise has a termination date. Along these lines, the cost of the option is additionally going to be affected by the lapse date. The closer you find a workable pace date, the lower the cost of the option – every single other thing being equivalent. A couple of days out from the termination date, the cost of the options never again get influenced when left until the option lapses. We call the decrease in cost from the time until the option terminates time to rot, and the worth that goes into the option from the measure of time left on the agreement is known as the extraneous worth.

The estimation of the option that originates from the hidden stock is known as the natural worth. In a perfect world, the inborn worth would come legitimately from the cost of the hidden offers. Keep in mind, there are 100 offers for an option agreement, so an ascent in the cost of the fundamental offer cost by $1 would mean a $100 ascend in the cost of the option. Likewise, a $1 drop in the offer cost would mean a drop in the cost of the option by $100.

In reality, the relationship isn't that simple, however, there is a number that you can take a gander at in stock information that will give you a decent gauge of how the cost of the option will change with changes in the fundamental offer cost. This is a Greek image called delta. It's a number that ranges somewhere in the range of 0.0 and 1.0, so on the off chance that Delta is 1.0, at that point, the adjustment in the cost of the option will be perfect that is a $1 ascend in share cost will bring about a $100 ascend in the cost of the option. On the off chance that Delta was 0.7, at that point the cost of the option would ascend to $70 for each $1 ascend in the cost of the stock.

The possibility of a call option is to give a bullish financial specialist, that is somebody who is anticipating the stock cost of some speculation to ascend in the close to term, the capacity to purchase portions of stock at a less expensive value that is settled upon already. So state that you claim 100 portions of a stock that is exchanging at $100. Perhaps a bullish speculator out there accepts that the stock cost is going to ascend to $105 an offer. In any case, they need a deal and they're just ready to pay $102 an offer. In this way, they can purchase a call option with that strike cost. On the off chance that whenever that the call option hasn't lapsed, the offer cost goes above $102 an offer, that would imply that the purchaser of the option could practice their privileges to purchase the offers. What's more, the vender of the offers would be committed to selling them at the limited cost of $102.

Presently, we should take a gander at it from vender's point of view. You might be bullish on the stock over the long haul; however, you may not trust it will pass $102 an offer. Additionally, odds include your repurchasing of the stock in the past at a lower cost than the present cost of exchange. In this manner, in the event that you needed to sell the offers at $102, you wouldn't be excessively annoyed, since you would presumably be making a benefit in any case – despite the fact that that benefit may be a considerable amount lower than the benefit that you would have made selling them at $105 an offer. In any case, as we'll find in a second, a portion of that distinction will be secured by the cash you get by selling the option.

An option isn't free. Somebody that needs an option is required to purchase it Cost per share is usually mentioned for an option. Along these lines, in the event that you look into the costs of options, you should duplicate the provided cost estimate by 100 to get the value somebody would really need to pay. We will take the example of our preferred profit stock, Abbvie.

The offer cost right now is $75.70. There are call options with strikes above and underneath this offer cost. For a call option, when the market cost of the offer goes over the strike cost for the call option, the cost of the option goes up by a great deal. Options with costs over the present offer cost are as yet worth cash (until they terminate), yet the higher you go in strike cost over the present market value, the lower the expense of the option.

Along these lines, we see a call option lapsing in three weeks that has a strike cost of $76.50, or $0.80 over the offer cost. It's assessed that there is a 69.7% possibility of benefit, implying that before the option terminates, the offer cost has a 69.7% possibility of being lower than the strike cost of $76.50. The cost is cited as $1.40

Owning 100 shares of Abbvie means that these shares could be sold for $140 as the share price is $1.4 and 100*$1.4 is $140 and each contract has 100 shares thus, ten contracts can be sold, having 1000 shares allowing to earn $1140. Premium is the payment for the options contracts which is the earning from stock including the profit while keeping the shares. However there are the risks of stock price going up to $77 per share, this will decrease the market price and you may have to sell shares at $76.50.

By picking a call option that has higher strike price can reduce the risks through making it less probable that shares have to be sold because of decreased chances of stock price reaching strike price or becoming more than it. The risks decrease with each higher strike price under consideration. It should not be forgotten that options expire and majority of them expire in the near term, which means that even after third or fourth week the shares are still with you. This is especially the case with stock like Abbvie which doesn't fluctuate much.

Therefore, for example that the share price reached $77 and share had to be sold for $76.50 or let's assume that if it goes up to $78.50 then $2 per share is lost. But these are the expected profits which are lost otherwise, you have lost nothing. If the shares were purchased in the past for example, in June 2017 and $67 per share was paid. For which reason they cannot be sold at$78.50 as it is higher price than the cost price. Moreover, the money earned from sale of an option contract belongs to an individual and you have earned $1.40 from this, when all of this is added it is approximately equal to$78.50.

Call option, in the language of option traders, is the money earned when market price of stock exceeds strike price of the option contract.

This situation won't concern you if the main reason behind trade of shares is the capital gains. But, there is a lot of risk that you might lose all your shares which will not allow you to earn dividend if you are dividend investor

Most traders want to earn surpluses through buying or selling options contracts. So, they are likely to sell options contract to other person if the option is being sold for a higher price than market price as this would ensure more profit.

Following are some prices of the money call options for Abbvie that end on the same day. A $75 call will be sold for $221 which is priced at $2.21. A $73 call will sold for $358 as it was priced at $3.58. This means that if there were 1000 shares then ten options could be sold for $3580 which is a great passive monthly income.

Dividend Stocks aren't Volatile

The main benefit of dividend stocks is that they are not unstable in this strategy. As a volatile stock has price swings which are quite disorderly and exceed the strike price, this can encourage selling your shares. Hence, majority of dividend stocks are stable and slow as they increase but at a slow and stable rate like, Tesla, Netflix, and Amazon, which means that there are lesser chances of selling your shares.

The risk of doing so can happen so, you must be careful while picking up the strike price that is bearable. If there is some discomfort in selling shares at$76.50 then you must pick $77 or any other price. But, it must be kept in mind that higher the strike price is the lesser amount of money will you earn.

You will earn more money if you go further out ore. High premiums can be earned from calls that will expire in the future. We can see that a $77.50 call could be sold for $4.73 per share, in this way when there are 100 shares per option an option can be sold for $473. If we had 1000 shares then 10 contracts could be sold for $4730.

You may go further out in time. An option is called a LEAP when it ends in more than nine months in future. This term stands for Long term Equity Anticipation Security. In case of Abbvie, a year and half into the future can be seen and it can be noticed that a $77 call is sold for $11.28 as the price of the option contract is $1128 which is the product of 100 and $11.28. There are more chances that some might 'call' the option and press you to sell your shares if you have longer time until option expiry. Hence, you may pick a strike price which is more than the purchase price of the shares (the price you paid while buying shares)

Put Options

The risk of selling shares with the covered call option can be reduced by the use of put options. What are put options? A put option allows buyer to purchase shares of stock at specific price. Similarly as in call option, this price is called strike price. The option traders buy a put option for a stock that is expected to decrease, then if the stock goes down, they would buy hundred shares at cheap market price which they will exercise and sell to the writer of the contract of strike price this is one way of earning profits. The profit is the difference between strike and market price. Let's look at an example.

Let's assume that a stock can be traded at $100 per share. A put option with a strike price of $90 per share is purchased but you do not have the ownership of stock. Still you will go for it if you guess that the stock is in massive fall so you afford the stock. If the option is sold for $2 then the total price will be $200.

If the stock declines to a great extent even before the date of expiry as for clear understanding we can take following example that the stock falls to $40 per share and 100 shares are bought amounting to $4000 which is the product of $40 and 100.

However it can be exercised as a put option with a $90 strike price is owned. This means that shares can be sold for $90 per each share allowing earning $9000 as $90*100 = $9000. In this way, profit of $5000 can be earned through sale of shares. Premium of $200 is also paid for the put option hence, the total surplus amounts to $4800.

Though these numbers are quite strange but they clarify the example and the way how put options work and reason of people buying them.

As earlier in this book, we have discussed the ways of using put option as a kind of insurance (stated in theory).

Expiring Worthless

At the present time, if we are short of time and strike price is not in a positive position, which means that the option expires worthlessly. In case of call option, if the market price is lesser than the strike price, the option has no value or worth when it expires. This is because none will be willing to pay more than the amount (the strike price) than they have to pay on the open market. That's why they will not exercise the option in any situation.

In case of put option, when the share price exceeds the strike price at the time of expiration, then the option is expired worthlessly. The reason behind this is that the individual applying these options will have to sell them for a loss which is illogical

Selling in the Money Call Options

A way of earning profits through decline in the stock price can be noticed, however, there is also another method to earn profits from a fall in stock prices which uses covered calls also. This can be executed through selling a call which is currently in money. To develop an argument, we can say that there is a threat in next three weeks about Abbvie. If the current market price is $75.70 than a call option can be sold for $74 if a fall in share price is expected as when fall in stock price is predicted, the call option which is out of money won't worth anymore and the call option can be written but, the call option which is currently in money will be valuable as high premium can be charged. The price for that option is $2.85 which will be multiplied by 100 making $285. Similarly if there are 1000 shares then $2850 can be earned. You must pick the share price with which you are comfortable as if the share price doesn't result in dropping then you might be pressurized to sell shares. Fortunately, if it drops below the strike price, then the shares can be kept as well as $2850 can be earned from selling the option premium.

Summary

More money can be generated from shares through selling call options. But, the risk involved in it is that the option will be exercised however, at times options are not exercised. Most of the times the option contracts are not exercised as the option traders are looking for better opportunities to earn m ore profits through trading the option contracts in short run. These option contracts are quite valuable. Further, many traders are searching for ROI off the minor investments that are needed by options. On the other hand, the costs for traders can be increased as $221 is needed to buy a call option having a strike price of $75 for Abbvie; it would cost $7500 in totality as 1000 shares of stock at$75 have to be bought. Many times, the investor is not willing to invest money in buying shares and there is an order of magnitude difference between the price of shares and option.

Though, this strategy seems to be appealing but, there us great risk of selling share that may discourage many dividend investors however, it may be good for you.

CHAPTER 15

DISADVANTAGES OF INVESTING IN DIVIDEND-PAYING STOCKS

Everything in the world has pros and cons and dividend-paying stocks also have both the sides. Many of investors believe that all of money must not be invested in these sorts of stocks because there is always a need to diversify and become a trader for some time. If someone has main purpose of buying stocks us to hold them then, it must be known that the stock market is very dull. Investing in dividends is a good idea if you are satisfied with a stable income and does not aim to earn more and more. But, most of the people want to earn stunning income and explore adventures of trading. There are some disadvantages listed below or the reasons of why investing in dividends can become a mistake.

1) **Uncompensated Risk:** one of the major problems of implementing this method is that there are many investors who solely give attention to individual stock investing. It is quite a risky affair as a well known proverb says that don't put all your eggs in one basket. In order to reduce risks and spread them, an investor must be diversifying his portfolio. The uncompensated risk is the unrewarded risk that can be reduced easily through diversification. Investing in five or ten stocks is also very risky so a portfolio of ten or twenty stocks is a great idea. The risk can be diversified away through buying cheap, very-diversified index

fund (that the investor will simply not get compensated for it). So, there is no need to invest in stocks that have risks which won't be rewarded as investment can be all about risk control. But, picking up the right stocks is a tricky task and if you chose your own stocks then there will be considerable risks involved. There are very little chances of individual choosing the right stocks as even professional fail to do so perfectly.

2) **It does not give Attention to Total Return:** Majority of investors only take yield, dividend, and income on investment in to account when buying stocks and ignore the total return. If there are two stocks , one has the yield of 10% while other has no yield so obviously first option appears to more appealing and you will go for it but, this data can misguide as it is just on the surface. . Real Estate Investment Trusts is known for being these types of stocks. As the investors just got to know that the shares have the value of just $3 instead of $10 per each share , which is the original amount paid by investors despite of the fact that these shares have 8% yield. Total returns are most important though, a major part of yield is called as the return of principal.

3) **Confusion between Dividend Stocks and Bonds:** Dividend stocks must not be treated as bonds though, they are able to give a standard source of revenue. Uncertainty is a key feature of stock market that's why even successful and strong firms that pay dividends can become bankrupt. Dividends are completely different from bonds, which are considered as loans and they have to be returned plus interest is charged on them. The value of

dividends keeps on fluctuating so firms like GE can even cut their dividends to 1 cent a share. In 2008, when there were financial problems, many dividends were cut. More than 100 firms from S&P 500 cut down their dividends. But, the case of bonds is different, whose yield was kept and value was increased. The comparison between Vanguard Intermediate Treasury Fund in 2008 which increased with 13.49%, whilst the Vanguard High Yield Dividend ETF decreased with 32.73% is a very appropriate example as we can notice that these two cases are poles apart.

4) **Dividends are Tax Inefficient:** Mostly competent dividends are taxed at the rate lower than the normal income still; it is not a great option for investors to distribute dividends. Many companies do not pay dividends for example, Berkshire-Hathaway (Warren Buffett's Investment Fund). Investors can decide the time when to pay taxes on their shares from portfolio of a firm, if they do not pay dividends. Through sales of shares an investor can announce the need of dividends. But, when investors do not announce any income, there is no need to pay taxes.

5) **An Inefficient Method of getting a Value Tilt:** some investors would assume that a firm which is paying dividend can resolve the firm to give more attention to profits for its investors. Investors many times believe that dividends are more significant than any rise in share prices. They are also able to give the recent history that will clearly show the performance of dividend-paying stocks and general stocks, allowing comparing both of them and determining how well these stocks perform. However, they won't

be helpful in determining the reason behind this change in performance. This is because dividend-paying stocks were generally value stocks in the past, in the times when these value stocks had greater proceeds than the whole market. It is unclear that whether this overrun is due to investor's behavior, or due to increased risks (or because of both reasons), but it is quite obvious that the investors will guide their portfolio towards value stock in such a order that it is advantageous for them. These investors mostly use a Price to Books ratio to turn their investment(for value stocks) in to right track, as chasing high dividends is not the most appropriate way to achieve this target. The investor will likely be in a better position with a simple value index fund or an ETF instead if he chooses to prevent from foremost and uncompensated risk through purchasing an ETF or a low-cost dividend stock index fund. Investing in dividends is inevitable but, investors must buy at least 20 to 30 shares from different firms in order to diversify, give attention to the total proceeds, use dividends in an appropriate way and ensure that there are enough amounts left after the deductions of taxes. By spending in market index funds or in ETFs, some investors will be willing to buy the ownership of dividend-paying stocks. It is personal choice whether to choose them directly however, it is advisable to all the things stated above before choosing this strategy.

CHAPTER 16

MORE COMMON MISTAKES MADE BY INVESTORS WHEN INVESTING IN DIVIDENDS

If investment is done in incorrect manner, then the dividends may not guarantee profits. The investor has to follow few principals and reduce chances of errors in order to generate spectacular amount of income and increase significantly the value of stocks over a time period. Following are these principles:

1) **Looking for Towering Yields:** it might be perceived that the stocks that are functioning well are the ones which haves highest yields however, this is not the case because it is quite difficult to stabilize high dividends which are mostly very unsteady. For the growth and development there can financial crisis so, experts suggest to not to rely on very high yields and recommend to check dividend payout ratios too. As many researchers have suggested that most effective stocks are the ones that have low payout ratios and dividends yield that are not soaring very much. The best spot for payout ratio is between range of 30% to 60%, according to David Ruff, that is the percentage at which firms can distribute dividends to the shareholders in a routine and such ratios can be easily plowed back into the stocks for a firm to grow internally.

2) **Having Mechanical Strategies:** the strategies must not be established on the largest numbers, as very high dividend payout ratios are unsteady so, you should not be blinded by such stock, which seem to be very appealing or have soaring dividend payout ratios, and hurry to purchase such stocks as more data is needed to examine these. Thus, these sorts of stocks must be evaded.

3) **Ignoring Factors Contributing to Growth:** rather than just considering dividend yield other factors like, capital appreciation and potential dividend growth must also be given attention as they are major factors that must be considered by investors before investing. For example, if the investor has $1 million in his portfolio and he wants to withdraw $50000 every year to pay for his costs of living. With just a 3% annual total return in 20 years, the investor would have less than half of his preliminary amount of $1 million, whilst another investor would have more than $1.8 million with an annual total return of 7%. In 30 years, the investor with 3% in annual return will reduce the money, at the same time as the other one would have more than $3 million. The above example highlights the significance of potential dividend growth and appreciation and why they must be examined.

4) **Focusing just on Domestic Market:** There is no rule prohibiting to invest in markets other than home market so, markets that are in better economic conditions and yielding better returns must be searched at home or abroad. The

average dividend yields are probably higher in foreign country with stock valuation that can be more beneficial.

5) **Blue-Chip Tunnel Vision:** Like in a poker table there are table chips of various colors. There are white, red chips as well but the blue chip is the most important. Thus, Blue-chip firms are the most celebrated and profiteering one. That's why these stocks are very costly and lower gains than mid- or even small-cap dividend payers. Though, investors are more interested in investing in large and well known firms.

6) **Following the Herd:** As stated above the large firms are not the most successful ones but, still most of the investors are willing to invest in the huge large-cap stocks in the market. This trend must be ignored and small and mid-caps stocks must be found, which are more effective than large-cap stocks. You should not make the same mistake as other investors made of not considering ability of unpopular stocks.

7) **Giving Macro Factors too much Attention:** other markets or the rising ones must not be ignored due to the reason that their respective economies are facing hard times s it does not mean that these they are no successful companies in these markets, these are the firm that have ability. Moreover, the world has been globalized and such company can easily export or provides its services to foreign companies then, the firm can still perform well in spite of political or economic stability.

8) **Looking for Dividends in Wrong Places:** Many times, people who are willing to spend in the stock market and also have substantial amount of earnings from dividends are usually looking for them in wrong direction. It is very complicated for them to achieve this objective, as they have not selected the appropriate field of activity or sectors. A general mistake these investors commit is that they search for very high-tech companies to invest in but, they fail to realize that the main motive of such firms is to expand and grow for this reason; they do not pay generous dividends. People mostly invest in such unattractive firms in terms of dividend payout ratio as they are attracted towards the brand image these firms have. It is similar to the investment in safe bonds because they don't have the highest returns. Investors must be searching for various opportunities and there is need to look outside the S&P 500. Firstly, the sector of activity must be chosen which must be the "hot" one and after it, best firms to invest in must be searched in the selected sector. For more charitable dividends small and mid-cap stocks must be preferred. The Dividend Aristocrats list can also be checked as it is the most excellent source for such stocks.

9) **Not Reinvesting in Dividend Payments when Possible:** Some shareholders may consider leaving this strategy as they are not pleased with the dividends they get. Because of this, they spend money earned from dividends on other things like, various living expenses, or purchasing stocks for trading

purpose. Still, reinvesting in the stocks will amplify the number of shares you currently possess. To conclude, it is said that more shares will be more the earning will be, as you will have more dividends. Reinvesting the dividends is always suggested as it is the best and most secure way to boost passive income.

10) **Miscalculating your Financial Need:** Purchase of stocks is a risky affair. You should not make decisions hurriedly even if you need money urgently, as it must be considered that dividend payouts should not swap with your income and also cover your living expenses. Special attention must be given to the accuracy of numbers; as if they are miscalculated then the affects are very distressing because overstatement of income and understatement of costs may happen. So careful future planning is vital for this strategy and the bar must not be very high that it will increase chances of failure.

11) **Misusing Dividend Strategy:** Most of the people will implement the technique which assures overwhelming results as they are usually appealed by big numbers. But, this strategy may become a failure, as when the expectations are set very high then, there is possibility of crash, so you should design your own strategy, which suits you when it comes to investing in dividend-paying stocks because choosing wrong strategy can have adverse effects. Before selecting your own technique, you need to have a clear understand about you financial condition, the cash flow requirements, personal

statement of financial position because the risks involved in this strategy must be calculated.

12) **Trying Dividend Investing on your Own:** In the bizarre world of stocks only best can thrive. That's why many investors need guidance and expertise to survive in this world. When carrying out your research there is constant need for specialist to guide and help to evaluate numbers. The expert can be your relative, or any professional who will show you the right way. But, it is vital for an expert to have a clear understanding about you aims, requirements and financial budget that you are willing to allocate on such investments. No one can forecast the future trends of a stock market due to the uncertainty but, you can easily achieve the preset targets and become successful investor with enough knowledge about stock market.

13) **Buying Stock based only on Hot Tip:** Without having enough and suitable research it is not possible to buy stocks merely because someone tells you to do so. It is suggested to hurry and buy stocks jumping on the offer (stock price) before the prices increase. This refers to act swiftly before evaluating the consequences. Thus, there is a possibility of buying stock without having crucial information about companies like DPR, PEG, and EPS. To execute this method, you must check financial statements and meet the representative of firm (or your broker at least) to verify whether the tip you got earlier was correct.

14) **Trading Shares just for Sake of Dividends:** there is a strategy where you buy stocks one day before the company pays dividends then after receiving dividend money you pay the shares at a very generous price. You win the money from dividends and from the difference in price. Though, it is very unpractical in real world, as if you successfully buy shares a day before dividend payout, you may not be able to sell shares at a good price, as the prices will fall after company openly announces big-time dividend payout. In this situation, the maximum gain you will receive is to break even.

15) **Buying Stocks just because they are Cheap:** For some investors the biggest achievement is to buy stocks at low prices but, there is a distinction between good value and low price per share because saying that share is cheap, does not mean that it was a good deal. That's why; buying stocks at lower rates is considered as gamble or speculation rather than investment. And, it must be questioned that whether cheap shares can help to earn money? Mostly cheap shares are related to the unknown companies. There is not enough information available about these companies. So, until you properly assess financial statements and some obvious indicators it is recommended not hurriedly buy cheap shares.

16) **Holding to Poor Performing Stock for Way too long:** the main agenda behind investing in dividends for holding stocks is to earn money. Though, it does not mean that you have to hold on it in every condition or forever. If you have bought

the stock which does not generate enough revenue, then you should free yourself from it. It is referred to as a losing strategy when you keep the stock hoping that it will generate income in future. When you are adamant not to let the stock go because of emotional attachment then, this attachment can be your most dangerous rival and you have to finish your losses and sell these stocks as it is an expense of stock but you will gain money in return. Now you must move on and invest in other stocks.

17) **Failing to Account for Taxes properly:** it is impressive to focus on ways to earn money through stock market but, some investors focus more on keeping money tied up as lower taxes are to be paid on the revenue that is generated from stock market. A qualified accountant can calculate the difference. You may earn $200,000 and pay 35 percent in taxes, so you remain with $130,000. If you pay only 15 percent taxes, you can walk off with $170,000. Thus, it is essential to have a qualified accountant with you as you can safe more money after having sufficient information.

18) **Giving too much Credit to Analysis and Media Reports:** Like other fields, stock market can have its own media. There are many channels, websites, magazines, television and radio shows associated with this topic. Some sources of information are very appropriate while some can entirely inappropriate as, some analysts exaggerate in stock market, so there is no need to worry and you must calmly find right information and

verify whether the news is real or not. You can continue with your dividend investing strategy if enough information backing analyst is found.

CONCLUSION

It must not be forgotten that through speculations and expectations you cannot "beat the market". Being a submissive investor, the increasing dividend is vital for the whole mechanism. As it will produce more money making you richer and protect from inflation; all you need to do is to plow back the dividends that were collected in companies that paid high dividends in a proper way. This technique relies heavily on decorum and endurance. Stock in your portfolio should be held conveniently and main strategy is to invest in dividend growth businesses and wait for the earnings.

It is essential to have an investment plan as it will protect you from following herd, designing wrong techniques or making decisions based on feelings. You must invest in quality companies who must be able to provide growing dividends that is adjusted with inflation and give a long term investing opportunities. You can chose many companies but, the companies you select should have firm position in markets in which they function and should be able to expand with superb management and growing dividend history of minimum ten years where the dividend must rise after every two years.

These are the three products of company Procter & Gamble: Duracell batteries, Ariel laundry and Head & Shoulders Shampoo. This company has paid increasing dividends for many years. Like this, there are many firms that products are used for day to day activities. Their quality and business model is not a secret for anyone so, everyone will want to become a shareholder in these companies for self enrichment and growing dividends. You can easily choose the option of which you will want to be shareholder it can be from genetics Research Company and its favorite brand of laundry.

There is no reason to go off the dividend that is growing faster than inflation. On the other hand, ripe benefits of periods when the stock markets decrease the prices of quality firm to give them cost advantage. To spread risks it is important to diversify and it must be ensured that your revenue does not rely on a single sector. The goal is to earn wealth and sustain it as well. The dividends can be sold to companies that are cutting their dividends.

And never forget that being rich is not just about having money. It's also about being rich in spirit. Your success will not depend only on your ability to generate revenue streams. It will also be related to your attitude towards others. So stay generous once you become rich.

Combining return, performance and lower instability of a stock portfolio can provide the selection of sustainable and growing dividend companies. The stock will rise as much as it dividend revenue. The strategy that is prescribed in this book has been implemented by investors of all ages in United States and Canada or whether it is a supplement income for retirement or to achieve financial autonomy.

It must not be thought that being rich is about having enough money. Rich is the one who is free spirited as the success is not dependent on potential to generate revenue but, also on the conduct towards others. So it is advised to be charitable after becoming wealthy.